A Museum of Moments
Vol III

Reflections - Emotions - Observations

A Trilogy

To Aunt Jean,

all my love

This paperback edition published 2020 by Jasami Publishing Ltd
an imprint of Jasami Publishing Ltd
Glasgow, Scotland
https://jasamipublishingltd.com

ISBN 978-1-913798-13-0

Preface

"These are my photographs; my snapshots"

I had an incredible life growing up with a very loving family and a varied circle of close friends. Life could not have been any better.

Then suddenly, at the age of fifteen everything changed in what seemed to the adolescent me a rapid succession of non-stop loss, a lot of which is detailed in these poems. The end result was an irreconcilable change both in me and in how I viewed life.

In order to deal or rather not deal with all the pain and emotional turmoil, I turned inward, locking out everything and everyone and turned to writing in order to deal with my thoughts, emotions, and hurt. Writing as opposed to talking or facing people made it all seem much easier - more remote and distant, and ultimately easier to deal with.

These poems make up all the things I never said to parents, to friends, to loved ones. and to lost ones. They are snapshots of memories that define a life - my life and I would like to think that some return has been made to those still reading on past book one, and will hopefully show that no matter what we feel, we are never truly alone.

"A museum of Moments, there but to parade." - Andy

Acknowledgements

Fine Art Photographer - Cover

John McIntosh

Jasami Publishing, Ltd

Thank you for continuing to believe in me.

Dedication

Once Again... For My Family

Foreword

This third volume of Andrew Wilson's poetry is once again being published in the middle of the first global pandemic in a century. This volume also contains several astute observations regarding global views which will resonate with every person.

Andy's Foreword details the origination of these three volumes of poetry. Every poem reflects his life and the myriad of emotions they evoke are an illustration of the resilience of human nature, that is so imperative in current society.

I hope that as you read you enjoy the expressiveness and eloquence of his language.

Michèle Bernadette Smith
Jasami Publishing Ltd.
November 2020

Table of Contents

A Close Shave

The razor opened; it laughed… maniacal
The flash of an idea reflected in the flash of a blade.
Ok.
Sweaty hands, erratic eyes, the thump-thump of a leaden chest.
Quick! Cold water on tortured skin; shaving foam to blot out an idea.

I heard you call.
From the hall
But I needed time to decide
Cold. Cold.
Water on face to stun my disgrace.
I had an idea.

You turn up the volume
From downstairs
A time to love?
A time to choose?
Maybe that's the idea.

Towel dry. Halt to watch it flow!
Then a piece; one tiny piece
Of toilet paper to stem the blood.
Cold water to stun a maniacal laugh
I heard you call.

It's ok; I chose the shave.

Andy 05.07.20

A Drink

How do you know when you're dead?
Do the letters stop coming? Do people stop calling?
And when the phone rings, and it's never for you
Do you accept the fact you're in the dark and just roll over?

Yet the drink still tastes the same, after a while anyway.
The familiar smooth takes its time replacing the acid bite of old.
Fools you into thinking, "Maybe things have changed!"
Yet the mirage passes with the first swallow as I fall down again.

The last, final reminders that things did change vanish in liquid.
Yet define the change? The walls are different, the view altered
Yet the glass is the same, the colour the same, the taste is
{almost} the same.
The pain is the same.

As I down the final swallow I feel… What?
I feel the ice on my teeth telling me "The End!"
The final drop of bile slips down my tortured throat.
And again I see {almost} that I haven't forgotten the way.

The glass is full again, yet I am emptier still.
Why is that? The paradox remains. I fill up yet empty.
Why do I not grow fuller the more I put in?
I guess my glass is different, emptying as it fills!

With the second gone I find I no longer can say "No!"
The ability has vanished along with my sense of life
This simulated death that I force upon myself
Is, strangely enough, the only reminder I have that I'm alive!

Andy 06.04.00

A Life In The Day

How did life ever get to this?
I was young. I was free. I was overwhelmed with dreams
Now I am the caged beast you stare at with guilty eyes
At the money grabbing zoo.
Beaten down by over bearing eyes and angry, snapped commands
I can no longer feel the wild coursing through my veins.

Why? No chain binds me, yet I feel them none the less.
The water in my bowl is tepid and warm… is undrinkable.
Yet my palate can no longer recall the taste of fresh water.
I am burdened by the choices I made, by the inaction I faced
And by the people I met, all who stripped me one meal at a time
How did life ever get to this?

Choices and opportunities lay before me, unending.
Now, they have bottlenecked while I sit in unmoving traffic
Yelling at the others flying by me in the fast lane.
On my way to a meeting I do not want to end the life I do not want.
I spin on my axis with no preference where I stop.
I just want to stop!

Now I sit in a bar with a drink that I do not want.
My stomach rebels "No more! Please no more!"
I ignore the onslaught of bile that tears at me.
I down the glassful of liquid that no longer satisfies.
Did it ever? I am but an aqueduct for alcohol,
A thoroughfare to things I do not want!

In my work now. A place I cannot stand.
A place I left for pastures new, only to return.
Head bowed, dignity in pieces as I begged to come back.

Full circle now, back to the animal in the zoo.
Lights come on, show time as I play my part to moronic fools.
I wonder now, still, how far do I still have to fall…

Before I hit the bottom!

Andy 13.11.08

A Minor Rant

Have you ever spent a lifetime running?
Galloping away at full speed!
Only to discover, through the joy of irony
That where you were is exactly where you want to go?

I love irony! The way it takes the complete piss out of you.
That moment of sudden unwelcoming realisation,
When you get smacked on the back of the head by fate and its hammer.
Then stand and stare at what's happened, looking like a complete idiot!

If only we could take a quick look at what's ahead.
Maybe see a few alternatives before deciding.
But no, we're thrust forward by the onslaught of time
Made a mistake? Awww! Tough!! One way only! Keep moving!

Why does what we don't have, look far more appealing
That what it is we actually have?
I'm here but I'm not happy. I want to be there.
I'm there. Guess what? I'm not happy…ad infinitum!

What am I trying to say? I have no idea.
I'm still trying to see through the laughter of crying.
I've ran away my whole life, from everyone and everything
Yet everywhere I go has the exact same problem as before…

And what is the problem? I'm already there!

Andy 19.09.08

A Museum of Moments

A Museum of Moments

So again I am reminded of another memory faded to black.
Who I was has no place here as the past is rebuilt.
Frown upon me as an almost tear breaks cover.
Yapping barks from walls within serve to remind.

A glass is broken.
Little matter that it once stood testament to a time I almost forgot.
It's just broken glass. What matters?
My past is just a past in the multitude of millennia.

Who will remember?

But don't you see? It was once part of me; part of who I was!
A million memories served up a pint at a time
Until it lay, solemn upon the shelf.
A museum of moments, there to parade,

Until idiocy and carelessness took it all away.

But perhaps it was just a glass
And the fragments no longer matter
Doubtless I could fit into the cup once more
I am not who I was and who remains is but a ghost lost and unsure

Still. The glass was something; was someone.
Maybe I am that glass.
Fragmented, broken, cast aside by a brutal brush and shovel
But don't you see…We once were whole.

Andy 24.07.13

A Whale of A Time

Oh look.
Another diet plan
Laid to waist.
And no, it is not spelled incorrectly.

You see, I ate it.
Ran out of crisps, of chocolate.
I ate them too.
And swallowed down the hope.

As the months count down
The scales count up.
Can't reach down to bury head in sand
So I'll just have second helpings instead

Running out of whales to simile
Same time I run out of trousers
Of shirts
Of excuses.

"O mighty god, no more! No more!"

Right men!
Load up the ship!
Ready the sail!
Prepare the blunderbuses!

We got a whale to kill!

Andy 07.07.17
This time!

Alone I Walk

Some days the pain is worse
And attempts to hide it fail.
Those days even love becomes painful.
Then I think "Why go on".

Should I, I wonder, carry on
Or remove the pain forever.
Am I then being selfish?
Refusing demands of others to become "me"?

Alone, alone I will wail!
Too much pain for one alone.
Even the fresh blue sky
Fills blood red, yearning for release.

Ah, for freedom I can cry
Although reality is much more harsh.
The loneliness wells up in me
When all around I see `togetherness'

Maybe I'm just in too deep.
Too close to the point, being me.
Maybe I'm just a little insane
But then again, isn't everyone?

Andy 25.3.93

Anagrams

Damn you,
No really!
Damn you!
And damn me too!

Where am I?
Oceanic again?
Acids inflated
Again? Back to this?

Really?

Did I not climb
Back from that place?
There is no life as pain
Nudges towards.

An ending I do not control.

There is no control
When one is the bastard
In someone else's nightmare.

Paradoxes and anagrams, do you see?
They define what I've become
Translations available upon request

As soon as I understand your motive.

I'm trying so hard not to say what I need to say,
But when volcanos erupt, it's hard to write words that are edited molten

I guess I'm not ready
Back I go into shadow and denial
I try but find sadly, all my efforts mugged

Until then, I guess, like some dead notion twit
I'll find some other way
To get my message across.

Andy 11.07.20

Anger Mismanagement

So we fixed it did we?
For a time.
Calm restored, sun rising,
Moonlit waters calm, clouds parting…
How many more cheap platitudes can I spawn?
What drivel pours from my condescending mouth,
In a second of love-induced idiocy?
Moronic more like!

Let's see. What else can I use?
Choppy seas? Calm before the storm? Love conquers all?
Ha! I spit in the face of my idealistic rhetoric!
I drone on and on so much I make myself sick!
We have love! We can overcome! We are truly love-evolved!
Truth is I grow tired of sycophantically pleasing my ego.
Look everyone! Look who I conquered! See here the timeless beauty!
Here, by my side… the face that launched a thousand mid-life crises!

No one turns. No one looks. No one notices. No one cares,
To see the idealistic goddess persona I created all in your image.
Perfection over reality; desire over common sense; lie over truth.
No change there then!
The way I live my life constantly confuses and astounds those around me.
How do I do it? Simple: 50 years! Yeah that's right 50 years,
Because in 50 years none of this will matter a damn,
I will be but a bitter remnant, a fragment stuck in someone's throat.

Nothing more than a memory there but to amuse,
50 years and my bitter, ballistic, botched, battered and balsamic

Personality will no longer try the patience of saints,
Or rip wives from husbands, mothers from children or parents from sleep.
Mere mild debris left behind by an ill-fated passing storm,
Forgotten in all but anniversary; a sad pause to lament the death of a dreamer,
The passing of a rule breaker; the loss of a son, a partner, a lover, an enemy,
A colleague, a rival, a neighbour… the list is endless oh ruler… the list is endless!

Andy 03.04.09

Another Look

I don't understand what I'm supposed to do.
Nothing makes sense, I don't have a clue
Of what my life is meant to represent
I'm not even sure of my own intent.

Who makes the rules and who sets the pace?
I was never formally told I had entered the race!
Who determines my life, my choices, my fate?
Am I really the fearsome hunter, or just the fucking bait?

I'm drowning slowly in choices I had to take
Without any clear visions, some choices were fake.
I rolled the dice and fell down the god-damned snake
Now again I find myself burdened by choices I have to make.

My mind is closing in on itself as I try to postpone,
Yet my subconscious goes on in a monotonous tone.
Forcing me to always consider and think of what I've done,
Making me spit out empty promises with an acid like tongue.

"I wish, I wish!" it's all I ever seem to say
Wishing there was some way out of this stupid one-man play.
I hate who I was and now I hate what I've become,
Wishing only for someone special to make me feel numb.

Who I am will forever give me grief
And even I can no longer see what's underneath
This stupid false image I give to the people I sought
While under my façade, my soul gives way to rot!

Andy 27.05.08

Betrayed

Again, again and again!
How many times is it now?
Why is it that you can't answer?
Is it that you just don't care!

I have tried so many times
To make you realise what you've done
Yet, as usual you cannot comprehend it
"It's my life" you say, again, and again.

I try so hard,
To protect myself from you,
Yet you always get inside me
When I shut the doors and dream.

The midnight hours take me
Filling my head with ideas
Of allowing myself to love you again
And I can't control them any more.

Why is it that you can't see it?
The misty shadows on your eyes,
Make it too hard for you to see,
So you again stumble blindly over me.

The dreams of you, they take me
Growing more intense each day
Yet the pain I associate with you
Casts its evil reminders over them.

I promise I'll try to break away from you,
After all, it's what you want for yourself
"Good!" you cry in elation, as once more I fall
Still hearing the word I always hear "Betrayed!"

Andy 06.12.93

Between Three Worlds

I am trying to imagine and recall the places I have been.
Along with everything that vanished in those crazy days.
I am becoming far more than I could ever conceive of yesterday
And through inaction risk becoming far less than I was at nine this morning!

My mind has turned in strange ways, I can see that now.
I threw away the familiar and kept only my omnipresent confusion
I couldn't look left nor right, or forward or back without seeing
Some lost part of me falling, slipping away, thou was it accidental? Or designed?

As always, I have two feet yet they stand not together
They stand apart a foot each in two worlds, now with a third on the horizon!
Beneath me lies my perfectly crafted abyss, still growing wider each day
I have unenviable choices: jump to left or to right? Fall into the abyss or find the third

"I had perfected a vision that told my soul the truth" - Lies! All lies as usual!
My soul has turned away, sickened and still I can find no trace of it.
"It’s not that I lie all the time, it’s not that at all!" yeah right!
Can’t decide? Heads or tails? Black or white? Right or left? blah, blah, blah!

Between my three hand crafted worlds is not a pleasant place to be
Nothing makes sense, indecision and anger remain my constant companions!

Why has this happened again? Why must I continue adding new worlds?
No closer to final choice, so I hesitate, stuck between crossroads and planets!

Andy 27.07.08

Bitter Cause

I take a step into a world where I honestly don't belong
I try to speak different with a new voice, a new song.
And I side step from the track where I currently reside
Only now there is no back up, no place to hide
And I smile and I try to play the game with no rules
Only I can't remember the format and I don't have the tools.

So I try instead to act like it don't bother me one bit
I laugh and I cry and I learn to say "shit!"
And I make believe, convincing even myself
For one single moment I'm me come down from my shelf
Where I have hidden away adopting society
To look confused at myself wondering why I cry.

But with the moon become shadow in the grip of a new day
I again become stupor with no words to say.
And with the memory remaining of what I was
I let slip on the reigns of my brief and forgotten cause.
So I again welcome the day when I know who I am
No matter though, that we both know it to be sham.

Should I thank you for this foray into my mind?
Should I dig deeper, worrying over what's still to find?
Or do I instead turn away with a grimace of sheer disgust
Over what was already there hidden deep in layers of dust.
And with realisation inherent to wake me in my bed
I realise you know more than I what lies beneath my head!

Andy 24.09.01

Bleeding

All alone now and bleeding from within.
Thought I had a chance, a way to finally win.
Now through the pain comes a new understanding,
A bleeding wound, slowly demanding.

What did you see when you turned and left me there?
Could you even grasp the depth of my despair?
The callous mind set, my lasting memory
Of all the things I never got to say.

You told me once that I was there for you,
I have no way to tell what lies were true.
I only wish I listened more to what was said,
Not ignored the growing fear and dread.

All alone now with nothing left to do.
Is this it? Is my life really through?
I just stand here alone in my pain,
I can't believe I'm right back here again.

Just a fool who will never understand,
The way that fate plays its gambling hand.
Let me go, I'm too weak to choose
If I stay here, I will always lose.

It's not enough to see me all the way through,
Yet still I am torn over just what to do
Am I where I am meant to be?
If that's true, why do I yearn to break out and be free?

Andy 08.12.09

Born

When I was born
I was worshipped, played with, displayed.
Then they waited while I learned.
They wanted me to speak.
Simple words like"daddy", "mummy".

I did.

And they cheered.
I stood, and fell. And I stood again
I walked and I ran, and I laughed.
Again they cheered.
I learned to smile for that cheer.

Dressed to learn. School tie, blazer.
Off you go, son. Learn to fit in.
One plus one is two; don't ask why!
Stand in line, recite, write.
Listen, don't talk!

"Happy thirteenth!

More cheers!
I still don't know why.
Celebrate that I survived another year?
Teens - A time to rebel while I learn to be me.
Then told to stop. "You must fit in!"
I don't want to fit in!

Twenties.

Convinced I know all.
"In time all children must kill their parents!"
I am aware! You're all wrong, I know best.
I strut, marking territory to find a place - mine!
The world is confusing. I'm scared. Help me, Mum?

Thirties.

Ah better! I am become a man.
I have seen, I have learned; I am me.
I look back with shakes of a head. "Was that me?"
The world is a friend upon whom I can trust.
I learn to hide my hates and I learn who to love.

So why do I find my forties so mad?
I am over rebellion, I am over hubris, I am over-thought.
Yet again comes the madness from I know not where.
I learn, after all that I have never learned.
Was all I have ever been but an illusion?
A mask to hide the fact I am still a page unwritten?

I see people - whole people, not fragments like me.
I am broken into so many pieces I can never be whole.
I seethe at those perfect people.
The ones I can never be.
Too long I hid the emotions I thought would control
Not realising the whole time they were learning me.

I don't know who I am.

I don't know who I want to be.
And so I remain
Broken, fragmented.
Held together by disillusioned truth
Over the promise of a tomorrow
That will never come.

All this - when I was born?

Andy 22.08.20

Break of Dawn

The dawn of today!
Will I see you
From across the chasm.
You on your side
And me on mine.

Today I can barely see you.
The chasm has again grown.
Stretching us apart even more.
Lonely hands desperately hope
To touch your distant love.

A love beyond the chasm.
Beyond where I cannot come.
Why! I scream
No one hears my silent scream
But me. I feel its painful sting.

The sunset of today.
I dream, I pray, I fear, I love
And think once more
Of our growing chasm
Desperately hoping to stub its growth.

Oh for too long I hoped!!!
Yet still I hope, in vain.
The tides of time pass so quickly.
I shall ignore them as I always have
Forever screaming my unheard screams.

Andy 17.07.93

Broken Chains

I have set my soul adrift on a sea of uncertainty.
As I cut loose the chains of my own design.
They fall, stripped of their power to haunt.
And like a newborn infant, I suck upon my first breath.

Those around me look confused as they hear the chains fall.
What is that? They cry! What does it mean newborn? Breath?
They have forgotten they were once alive, that they too can run
Yet they blank me with stares as the chains consume memory.

I can jump, I can see, I can think! I can drop the act!
At last I have the silence, the voiceless peace that I craved
The chance for quiet, no voices any more yelling, demanding.
And the money filled men still do not know who I was.

I can look to the future with eyes open, without a custom grimace
Can at last envision hope with my new-found breath and peace
What lies tomorrow? Next week or next year?
Who knows? Who cares? But who understands my lack of fear?

The chained will watch me leave, care free.
What will they feel? Can they feel?
They will not have time to breathe, to consider
For the voices will yell and never notice I'm not there!

The condemned will go on, no doubt of that
In time they will not even remember the heretic who refused.
Refused to believe that the voices know it all.
"We must obey!" they will cry as the chains suck away even their tears

With breath in my lungs, and blissful silence within

I walk the familiar street with ease for the final time
I will not look back, will not think of the voices
That yelled, more! More! And consumed my soul from within.

It's all gone!
Finally!
They're gone!
At last I can be me!

Andy 20.07.00

Dedicated to so many people: To the colleagues that I leave behind (You all know who you are), to the voices that gave me the material for this and for Down, Down (Check it out, this is the sequel)

And once again to my family, for having the courage to believe in me and for allowing me the chance.

Control, Alt, Delete

There are times when I've wondered
If I am what was expected.
Or if I am little more than a flawed conclusion
To pre-planned equation.

If I am all wrong, then what's to be done?
There's no way to reboot the brain.
I am here, there's nothing more I can do,
Except soldier on searching for The Answer.

In my 30's now. Still no closer to the solution.
I am in many ways even more confused these days.
My 10's were fun, the world still fresh, my 20's insane, inane.
I wonder now, what can I expect from the rest?

Turn me back to little un-programmed infant.
Let me look again, maybe this time I'll get it.
This confusing, insane and cryptic life
That has left others smarter than me scratching their heads.

I have lived through so many dreams that little remain.
I have been a rock star, a movie star, a poet and a Boss.
Yet I'd like to let you in on a little secret,
Even I can't figure out the fact from the fiction.

So can I do it all over again? Make changes?
Most things in life can be remade, rethought, rebooted.
We can write a complaint, get given a better one.
But what of me? Version 1.0, stuck, immobile, confused.

I'd like to "control, alt, delete" my whole bloody life!

If I knew back then what I knew now…
Yeah, right, I'd probably repeat the crap I did so many times,
Little doubt of that, but what's a 21st Century digitised guy to do?

Andy 18.09.06

Crossroads

Crossroads

Standing at the crossroads, the all too familiar path before me once again,
This time is unlike the others, there are no set answers on which to depend.
To the left lies safety, laced with promises I've already seen,
To the right lies the danger, envisioned only in my midnight dream.

I feel life surge through me, it penetrates my nearly dead skin,
The cause of which lays submerged, buried deep in sin.
Veiled insinuations that quietly push me in a different direction,
Who could understand my reasons? Who would understand my defection?

My chest beats faster, fuelled by hints thrown subtly my way.
But still I am wary, fearful of things we never got to say.
Memories collide now in a sickening conflict of vision
And I am unable to conclude; to make my final decision.

Shall I pause to lament then, wishing I had stayed away from temptation?
But what good would it do, to simply force myself to deprivation?
I had one moment to choose, to lift me from my self imposed lament
But I blew it, and now the grass below me has changed to unyielding cement.

I was more alive in those five minutes and will spend years trying to recover,
You took away all my pain, showed me there are more wonders yet to discover.
And I didn't get to thank you for reminding me I live,

But now must forget what you showed me, ignore all you can give.

Should our paths collide once more, then perhaps I'll try again
Tell you to your face, in the moment, not cowardly with cryptic paper and pen,
It's useless now to play the what-ifs from within the safety of my head,
I can no longer settle for fiction, when you're out there offering reality instead!

Andy 09.12.03

Cruise Control

Mental state in decline
Cruise control.
Too long in the mire.
My skin is not my own.

I am open. Too open.
I took blackened, ruined parts of myself.
Unused for way too long.
And unleashed nerve endings; there is pain.

You do things outside of what I know.
I react.
Instead of the dead and the silence
Comes the hurricane.

I am sorry.

I see me from the corner.
Flaming eyes and vile remonstrance,
Venom I never knew smothers reason.
And all I can do is stare.

And

Bring the shame and voice the whispers
I no longer fit my shell.
I don't know where to turn, what to say.
I destroy - It's what I do.

In my own rage I immolate.
Simmering in the dark I wonder.
I feel what I cannot afford and I fall
Rot at the core, spreading ever outward

Vapours are all that remain.
Whispers of the man I used to be.
Fragments of moments ingrained in walls.
Who saw me fall? Who saw it all?

Andy 30.08.12

Don't Let Them See

Please don't leave me on my own
I can't handle being alone
Too many thoughts race through my brain
None are good enough to help keep me sane!

The walls close in and the ceilings attack
I don't know how I'm supposed to fight back
I'm running and hiding, and I can't get free
Everybody's pointing and yelling at me.

Please don't leave me here all alone
I can't handle me on my own
React me, distract me, from being me
Don't let my demons see what I see.

I can't handle this, I'm all alone
Petrified and terrified and turning to stone
Show me the blue sky that's hidden from view
The only time I see it is when I'm with you.

I don't want to be the only one left dying here
Living and drinking and dining on fear
I may look like I'm tough; a real hard guy
I'm just the coward who's waiting to die.

Don't let them see me when I'm all alone
Cowering in bed with a whimper and a moan
As night fades and the dawn turns to day
Please, someone, make it all go away!

If you can't, or if you're unable
Then give me a moment to practice being stable
If there's one thing I've learned from my evolution

Is the art of perfecting a believable illusion.

“Good morning! Isn’t it a beautiful day?”

Andy 21.08.20 (Finished)

Electric Chair

Strapped into a chair of my own design,
The restraint? Well, that was mine.
The juice was poised, ready to flow.
Little doubt I would have survived the blow.

I drove the long mile wondering what to expect
Ignoring the fact that my dreams are circumspect
Hands gripped the wheel and sweat formed on my brow
Living not for the future, or past, but for the now.

I knocked the door, with my heart pounding loud
Expecting the glares of my assembled crowd.
The door opened to show eyes I cannot ignore
And my beating heart increased to a roar.

In I came, to sit on the bed,
Wondering if I should run instead.
Yet my feet would not move, I was glued to the floor
Not enough strength or will to reach the door.

Transfixed by that smile that stops me dead,
So many thoughts race straight past my head.
My palms sweat, my mouth opens to talk
Powerless to speak, as I begin to walk.

Silence in the air as the condemned stands alone,
Forgetting everything he has ever known.
Life compressed into this once single breath
Does he have enough strength, to see past death?

I felt the electric charge as it slammed into me
Overwhelmed by the sensation, I could not see.
I used all I had to remain standing, and not fall,

And now my mind is forever locked in that hall.

And now I sit, alone with a stupid grin on my face
My heart is just beginning its come down from the race.
I feel regret coursing through me, an opportunity missed
We could have done more, and not just….

Hmmm.

Andy 21.12.06

Evolution

Never before had I even realised,
The blinding source of life you give,
To everyone but yourself. You lie and cry
Alone with your pillow, while we turn away
Unseeing in your time of greatest need.
What am I doing? What are we doing?

If I promised to give you more than I do,
Would you even believe the serpent
As he tries to cover the falsehoods
That spill from such a tainted mouth?
Could you even forgive the unknown lies
That hide under every morsel of truth?

Would it perhaps, be possible
To believe me when I say I didn't mean it?
Didn't mean the hurt that screams
From my every action as I go on with today?
Are you able to see past the ugly outside?
Into the warmth that sleeps within?

You don't know it, but I feel the sting
Of my words as they cut deep into you
With their painful barbs that are my promises.
Each time I cut you, I tear myself a little.
With utter repent over my passed life and time,
You take away the dark every time you forgive.

What did I do to deserve a person like you?
I consider myself gifted beyond all others
Every time you smile and compliment me
On some trivial, little action I blindly make.
I think of the hard times I've caused you,

And wonder at your motives for returning for more.

I feel the warmth of your feelings even as I sleep,
They remain my ever-constant reminder and reason,
For waking up once again in the rainy mornings.
How can I ever repay this that you give so freely?
Everything I can do for you in return fades in comparison,
And once again, I am torn by the actions that are my life!

Andy 04.05.94

For you, Mum

Exit Strategy

The end...
So soon?

Too tired to sit by the wayside selling sad tales to apathetic strangers about the death of dreams.
Solemn is the midnight bell.

Bored of white-washing memories for the gratification of self while trying to cover scar-blackened moments of things long imagined and long yearned, only never were.

Who believes me anyway? Lipstick smiles and glittered eyes that flittered behind masked lies and truncated parables. Who is still listening?

People snigger as they point at the Egg who fell, only to land in manure that never blossomed. Perfumed ammonia fills this petty climax.

Iced tears that did not come signify another forgotten promise. Who laughs now? Fragrant are the hopes that fail and how bitter is the stench of their absence.

So this is just another end. One among many never lamented and ever imagined. I am tired. I am bored... And worst of all, I am still falling... falling.

I have no exit strategy; no answers.

How many barbs can one man bear? Wounds never healed are given to fester. Must old scars be cut once more to the solemnity of the psychosomatic?

For whom does the bell ring now?

Andy 19.03.12

Fade

Silence blankets the room.
Statues that do not speak.
We hold formless shapes unrelenting.

Esoteric burdens that we do not share
Corrode memories and unravel dreams.
Where are the tumbleweeds? They should be here.

Do I fear Fear more than you do? Do I abhor more?
Have we conjured nightmares from nothing?
Do we un-create creatively in our dramatics?

I don't want to play anymore. This game is not fun.
Where are the smiles, the elegant electricity of our fires?
I do not want to be the misanthropic man I make in my madness.

Do I dare hope? Can I find the way back?
Or has the bracken taken hold? Have I but bitter remnants?
Charred memories painfully hoarded while the madman mutters.

A prize worth fighting for? I remain convinced.
Unique in fact; unreal in fiction.
Truth – a sellable commodity. Open to interpret, open to abuse.

A solemn room, blanketed in silence.
Unrelenting statues, unforgettable stares.
They lie amid transient forms that fade in perfect twilight.

Andy 19.03.10

For Maggie… as always.

Family, Part IV

Were there times when I lived with any kind of joy?
Was there something more in long ago days than this, my present life?
Were there ever days when I paused, if only for a moment, to look around?
Did I ever cry out with blinding tears wondering why? Am I, in fact, still alive!

Tomorrow is my birthday and I can feel no love, cannot feel much of anything.
I don't care that I am growing older, because in truth, I can become no less.
Will the others around me cry out; possibly welcome my continued presence (absence?)
They are probably wondering why I am alive and still distant for another yesterday.

Who wonders what happens to me tomorrow? These days it is isn't me.
People tell me I have lost the will to enjoy even Today.
And what once I considered as joy has turned to bitter problem,
One that I cannot overcome even by hiding away for another year.

Tomorrow is my birthday, and I can't imagine its imminent effect.
New friends with new messages, where are the hidden frowns?
Who believes I have done everything wrong with my days.
I dread the effect; after all, I have enough pain to call on from memory.

So I thank you all for the anticipated generosity I believe is heading my way.

I am dragging my chains through similar paths, unsure of where I have to go.
I can hear you now, on my birthday, offering yet more opinions on change,
I stare with confusion: Which hand loves you, and which one offends?

I still dream the remembered sounds of Christmas songs,
Can visualise the stairs worn with love and can think of faces staring.
The presents you will hand over, the price, as always… my self-respect,
Yet I do not forget for one moment that you starved to give me those toys.

Will our extended family join us for a New Year toast to welcome time anew?
Into our homes, we go, offering hugs; gently grasping hands in lingering hope.
I will slip away from the dutiful laughter. I'm not an important part any more,
And will I notice I wonder, that there's no one at my dinner table once more?

Andy 10.05.07

Family Part V - Covid-19 Edition

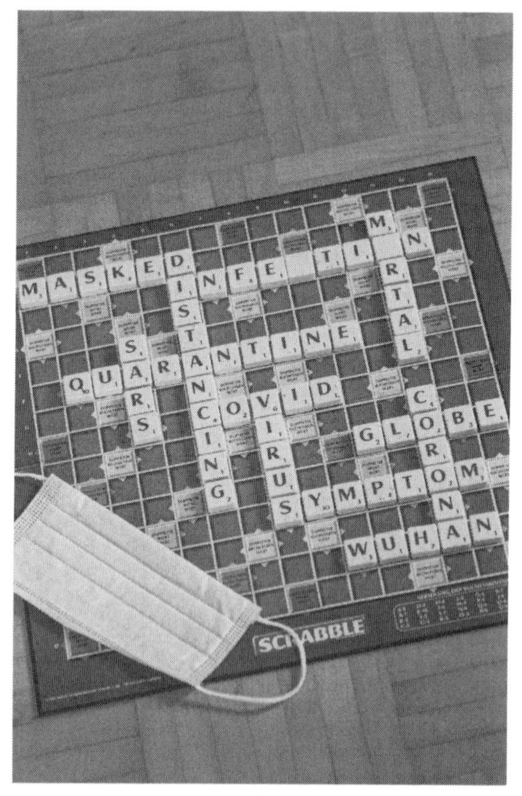

Family Part V - Covid-19 Edition

There were times when we lived with sovereign joy,
Much more than we do since the lockdown
These are the days when you look out the window
And cry out with blinding tears because you cannot visit the living.

Tomorrow is my birthday and already I feel its love.
It is not a time to worry over growing deaths caused by Covid-19
It is a time to protect those around us and cry out to welcome
The fact that we are alive and here despite the threat.

Who cares what happens right now. Who really cares?
We may have lost the joys of our every todays
As we self isolate to protect our tomorrow
Look at us as soldiers protecting our nations, rather than a problem
That forces us to hide in deep waters until it's gone.

Tomorrow is my birthday, and already I feel its effect.
Friends and loved ones cannot gather as isolation is still in effect.
Instead I have FaceTime Smiles that signify I am doing something right with my days.
I will feel the love, even when this Covid Pandemic has passed to memory.

I thank all of the Key Workers for the ever-present generosity you give to us
We cower indoors, unsure of where to go tomorrow,
Yet still you go to work so I can sit here and enjoy my birthday with tokens of love,
I try to give to my loving right hand and not offend with the left.

Hopefully we will all awake to the sound of Christmas songs,
coming from downstairs.
We will run down the worn stairs with love in our hearts to
accept;
To welcome the presents left to us after the full cost of of the
pandemic is finally revealed
Yet some will forget the fact that many died to give us our toys.

families will join for a New Year toast to welcome time
Into our very homes, we hug, shake grasping hands in love.
I promise to slip away from the happy singing to complete a
promise:
That never will I forget the empty spaces at the dinner tables of
those who died saving those who lived.

Andy 10.05.20

For all the heroes - The carers, Captain Tom, and all at the NHS: Thank you for keeping us all safe!

Feeling

My head opens up and words pour out.
People stare and ask what it's all about.
Sometimes, I tell them it's anger. Sometimes fear
It depends on the weather and the time of year.

I try to be cool and I try to keep it real
Yet sometimes, even I don't get what I feel.
I go to every corner of my little mind
Unsure in the end, and fearful of what I'll find.

I try to write down the thoughts that flow
Yet my feelings come so fast, and my writing slow,
So I end up just deciding to fake it
Wondering all along what would happen if I break it.

My mind is a mess, I don't know where to start.
It's like my soul is already packed, waiting to depart.
Am I just stopping here, or is this really my life?
A nine-to-five mortgage™, waiting in line for the wife?

I get so confused just trying to figure these things out
Just when I think I'm there, I forget what I'm about.
Who the hell thought emotions were the answer to the question?
I only wish they'd paused and given a moment's reflection.

Would it be better if I were unmovable, like the stone?
Just go where I'm taken, depending on where I was thrown.
I wish I could unload this crap that constantly fills my head,
And just get on with the job, not even noticing I'm already dead!

Andy 26.07.05

Flat Line

I should've asked for you to wait for me.
While I figure out who I am.
I wished I understood my reasons,
Instead of trying to break out of my own skin.

Would you have listened as I poured out more self deceit?
Would you have looked at me with more than sheer disgust?
Time will never tell me more than I already know right now:
I should never have died.

Slow burn suicide.
I'm on the one way hill, heading down.
My brakes dismantled.
I should never have chosen this path.

What would you say to the turned out few?
Would you be kind? Spreading whitewashed lies to spare broken hearts?
Or would you lay out the truth, black and brutal
To hell with who hurts?

I wouldn't blame you!
In fact I'd understand
I never thought myself capable of the agony I wrought.
Now I fall, submersed in clean cut guilt.

Dazed by untold secrets,
Bleeding from untold truths
And wishing I could take back what I sowed.
Too late… too late!

Too late, goes the bitter refrain as agonies of choice play their solemn tune

Through countless sleepless nights.
Haemorrhaging dreams and memories all to hollow words of regret.
Breathing slows, pulse weakens.

Pulled down by weights of decisions both painful and unending
Until in the end even my heart beat will succumb to a reality too hard to bear...
Thump... Thump... Thump.
Flat line!

Andy 07.06.09 (Finished)

Fragments

I wander at work
I'm frivolous with friends.
I moan at marriage
I'm lax at life.

In my world of banal
You stand there alone.
Like a million watt bulb,
In a room full of dark.

I blink and you're there
And open my eyes and you're not.
I sense you behind and when I turn round
There's nothing there but my back.

I moan when I'm happy
And laugh when I cry.
I'm at peace when I'm angry,
And bored when I'm content.

I wait for your call
And jump when it comes.
I can't wait to see you when I get home
But sometimes I'm there and you're not.

You're the sugar cube in life's bitter pot.
Without it, I could not drink.
Sometimes I find I miss the pungent black
When wonder why the hell is that?

I started this book, then found there's no end.
Someone has taken the last page.
Do I go back to the start, pay attention this time?

Or simply sit back and write my own conclusion?

Why am I laughing?
And why do I cry?
Where am I going?
And does God know why?

Andy 15.12.06

Hollow Voice

I can hear voices that ravage my brain They all talk at once to convince me I'm insane. They go on and on, never giving me a break, Until I feel that my very soul is up for the take.

No longer can I understand or see the beginning or the end, The place I split from me, the one on who I used to depend Now hear the story of the man who fell into a hole No longer complete, see me walk around un-whole.

The daily facade wears me down, no longer have I a choice No longer a vision of truth, just a burned out hollow voice. My reality no more than a fragile loose hold on what was real I am left unsure of what I saw, tasted, and can't trust what I feel.

I bring a blanket of nostalgia to try and help me keep my ground, I look for what I recognise only to find that there's no one around. So I envision a past that stood out from blurry truth, Scream out loud, and cry for my misspent hollow youth.

Where is the truth that once I believed? Where is the crystal clear? I cannot understand what's real, there's no one left to hear. So I am forced to speak to walls, to stars and to the very sky, Yet cannot comprehend why they don't understand me when I cry,

I split from truth so long ago, I don't remember where,
All I can do now is look to the past, sit quietly and stare.
Look for who remains, who loves me as I am now
As I unearth the distant memories and set forth with heavy plough.

Unclear as I am as to what I'm supposed to do,
I look at myself mirrored, and see me split in two,

One who seeks the glory of what's to come, but he's merely paediatric,
And the other I see stumbling, muttering, little more than geriatric.

Who sees me? Who knows me? Who wonders? Who believes? Who listens? Who understands? Who asks? And who the hell cares!??!!

Andy 18.11.02

How Long Will It Last?

I can't eat or sleep for worrying about the past
And fretting over the present, worrying how long it will last.
The pressures I bring to bear on my growing disgrace
Make me fear my own mirror; make me hide my scarred face.

Assailed on all sides by doubt and by debt,
And wondering silently, if the future is set?
Am I victim of choice or mere circumstance?
Did I offer myself feely? Or was I forced into this dance?

One more place that I don't want to be.
Ripping myself open, losing even more of me.
New rules, new laws and a new play to perform,
New faces to laugh and to gasp as my soul begins to deform.

I walk a new road, still wearing my old shoes
My demons have come with me, still march on in twos
I struggle to breathe and to grasp just what I'm about
Still fight and still lose to pain, rage, anger, fear and doubt.

Inner peace to me remains an unattainable goal,
Much like the desire to retain myself whole.
No matter what I have or will ultimately achieve,
I will still be left with the desire to just get up and leave.

Andy 07.04.09 (Finished)

I Found (Time)

Plans. Made yet taken
Away
By chance
Or as some might say
By design

I thought. That I'd see you
Friday
For that drink we promised.
But fate or predestination
Had you booked.

I'll do it!
Tomorrow.
That lunch we promised, procrastinated
I'll come see you, I love you. I promise!
Tomorrow.

Funeral booked.
Instead.
Because
Fate or predestination
Had you booked.

I've moved my plans.
Forward
A couple of years. Not yet.
Gotta deal with crap now.
Later! Ah, later!

Things will be amazing
Then.
Plans. Made. Yet taken

I had a chance.
I'm not ready!

I wasn't ready!
Too little time given
Too much time wasted.
I did love you; There just wasn't time.
I'm sorry. Truly I am; I couldn't find the time.

Tomorrow?
Day after Tomorrow?
Maybe Tuesday after next?
Definitely by the weekend.
I thought that I'd see...

You?

Where are you?

I found the time...

I found...

Oh!

Andy 25.05.17

If....

My mind darkens once more.
It flees from the happy
To shelter beneath dank dreams others would call nightmare.
In shadow I regret
And lick wounds made fresh again.

I cannot stomach the serene
And mackled ideals repel
Cover me in darkness
I abhor this sugary-sweet day.
Accuse me of tangent and deny my refute.
Who is the real anyway?

Perhaps I am stuck when I thought myself free
Maybe I yearned too much
Amid the altar of choice.
What if I were right and you were wrong?
What would happen then?

What
Would happen then?

Andy 23.2.15 (Finished)

I Want

The blood is not mine. The wounds are mine
I caused it, the fucking sublime!
I wanted to want to be just like you,
One of the pretty people I wished that I knew.

When heads turned and smiles were placed
I didn't want to be the only one disgraced.
I wanted to want to be just like you,
One of the chosen ones - the confident few.

Heads turn and shared glances pass
Idiots make comments both painful and crass
I dissolve into demon as punches come my way,
Overcome by rage at the things some people say.

I twist and slip, become more undone,
Less the real me; less my parents son.
Emotions take over as love plays its solemn song,
Leaves me with the guilty feeling I've done something wrong.

I just wanted to want to live like others do,
I found the way, but I cannot see it through.
For I no longer have the stomach, the strength or the desire
So I fall down charred by the flames of my own fire.

I wanted to want to really, honestly believe
Now in reality I wish I could just up and leave
I am not what was intended; I am not "The Man!"
And I remain as always, the one person I truly cannot stand!

Andy 29.11.09

Jumper

This morning I woke up at the bottom of the cliff.
Broken, confused, consumed, I lay in shock.
I tried to look up to where I was, yet saw only clouds
I cannot see the summit; the plateau I created.

Something happened in the dead of my night
That changed the course of my life.
Again, at 3am, I pulled a 180.
Then jumped without realising once again.

So here I lie, unable to move or to comprehend.
The white washed walls up there, gone now to ruin.
Images I made, created, believed in now twist and turn
And I no longer remember my reasons for climbing.

Pain is all I feel now, for the first time in years.
I opened my mind and soul to the power of my convictions.
Yet now I find thorns instead of roses, I force a dry tear.
I close my eyes to block the pain. It does not help.

Where can I go now? Try to climb again?
Maybe head down further, deeper to where I belong,
I can't make decisions like this; they've always made me
So I turn instead to my trusty friends. Shit, they've gone too!

What happened this time? Why am I lying cold and alone?
I've been here before, that doesn't bother me.
It's the fact I'm here again when this time I thought it was real!
Manufactured feelings, improvised love, make believe
memories…

Andy 17.06.08

Just Out of Reach

I brush my hair in the style that you say.
I wear my collar different; I button it your way.
I have learned to speak anew, I pretend
To listen as you talk, yet really do not comprehend.
And I cough with little finger raised
Yet still I walk squint and still remain dazed.

The mirror smirks as I brush my teeth
It alone is aware of what lies beneath
This false exterior that I wear all for your sake
It knows what I do not! That underneath, I'm still a fake!
For the truth is, I could easily slip down again, independent
And harbour yet more fears, more tears and even more resentment.

I have learned under duress how to play your damn games
I have studied your rules, your rites and your names
And I can smile when I need to, blurt out a reply
And can even convince myself when I really, really, try.
But when I lie in dark with collar loose and hair a mess
It's only then do the two sides meet and I feel distress.

So you see I do try to listen to what you teach
I guess that your vision of me remains just out of reach
And though I strive to live in the mould you have poured
I cannot commit myself fully as a member of your horde
And as I struggle to embrace your social reality
I'll either become as one with you, or just another fatality.

Andy 21.07.01

Just Stop

I'm Alive!

Free!

Loved

Choices!

Options - unexplored

Chances - unfulfilled

The sooner you kill me the better off I'll be

Past mistakes
Last mistakes?
No more mistakes!

Too many missed takes

Fettered

Unloved

No choice

Copy the 6th line.

Ignore the seventh?

Stop
Finding
Patterns

Stop
Finding
Hope

Sterile is the world
Where even dreams conform

Stop!

Patterning
Hope.

Just...

Stop.

Andy 26.06.18

Lockdown

I watched the talking heads today as they babbled and again changed their tune
Some say we're under control, others say it's too soon.
So as we head out of lockdown, will we pause to consider the real cost?
Not financially, who cares about that? What of all the people we lost?

I turned the tv off; I've heard all the nonsense before
Some want less of it all while others beg for more.
But did you notice today, that birdsong is louder and how the waters run clear?
Smog is lifting, and from my garden I can see faraway from here.

We realise we miss family far more than we miss money
Although there are some who'll laugh and find that funny
The billionaires sack their staff, worried their cash piles will run out
So beg the government for more! What's that all about?

We don't know what we have until it's all gone
Never been more true - we've known that all along
The world has stopped, we can all relax our grip
But be wary, the money-men are still there desperate to crack the whip.

So now the leaders worry that their bonus will be badly hit
So they rewrite the guidelines and rush to promote a new writ
"Get the people back to work, we need our country back on track!"
What they really mean is: "to hell with people! We want our money back!"

Will we learn from this lockdown, will we remember what we found?
That our leaders are meant to serve us, not the other way around
So before this ends and we all rush back, Slaves to the grind
Look a little farther; dig deeper - you never know what you'll find!

Andy 15.06.20

Dedicated to all those who lost their lives in the COVID-19 pandemic and all those who worked tirelessly to help others.

Made of Glass

Turn around.
Do you see the mirror?
It's supposed to be a reflection,
Not an alternate you.

I see my eyes, my face
Only they look alien now.
Words form, I can't make them out.
A frown forms, now that I understand!

Is it still me. In the mirror?
Perhaps an alternate version?
Does he have my worries, my hopes?
Is his life better, or merely duplicate?

Who is the reflection and who is the source?
Is he looking at his mirror and seeing me?
Where does he go when I walk away?
Am I the shadow that thinks itself the source?

I envy the reflection.
He's but a snap shot of today.
Blink, and he's gone. Vanished.
I remain, solid, liquid, skin, sand.

He is the mirror,
Yet I'm the one made of glass.
Cut to shards, pieces of mistakes
Fragments of what was, that never will.

Andy 26.09.06

My Allegory

Sometimes we bleed for the pain
And not just to be helped.
Sometimes we need the hurt
And not just to forgive
When I tear at my flesh
It's not done for you to gasp
Sometimes the pain itself
Is what's keeping me alive.

When you see me with spade in hand
Yet never see me dig
Do you wonder where the dirt goes?

And when you see me drop the reins
For the first time in my life
I don't need to see you panic
Or ask me why.

I know I've lost my place in this
I don't fit anywhere anymore
I did... for a time.
Ah! Now THERE was a moment!
If only I could've stayed!

People speak in words
That I cannot comprehend
And when people take and take

And I've nothing left but inculpatory silence
What choice did I have but to be bucolic?

Now do you see my true allegory?

Andy 20.08.20 (Finished)

My Goliath

I've wasted half my life chasing the dream they told me to.
I ran and ran, I fought and I climbed
A ladder that was never mine!
The closer I got the less I understood.

Somewhere back there, I got lost
Somewhere amid the myriad of choice
Lay the path destined - the one I overlooked
I didn't have the voice, nor the wherewithal to fight the bracken and claim what was mine.

So now I lie in the dark moments
Licking caustic wounds caused by falls that were never mine.
Lamentations and protestations never mine
Brought barbed arrows that never heal as I sit wondering why.

Was it treason to refuse to live the dream they never claimed?
Was there a choice overlooked?
When this David fought that Goliath I could only watch
Fearful of an outcome in which I would have to react.
Better to succumb to false promises than to prepare to follow one's own fate.

Now in a moment of perfect clarity do I see
I see what was done in my name when I had no vote
Secret societies and meetings brought cryptic policies sought to mold and build
But you dig too deep, do you see? Your hammers rang too loud

I know now, you know.

Now.

I know.

Andy 29.6.20

My Mistake

A while ago I made a reflection regarding me,
A suggestion that all is as I wanted it to be.
At the time I felt confused, alone, cast out.
Yet now I can see that it was merely self doubt.

When the time I loved most had gone to past.
I sat by myself, my flag lowered to half mast.
I felt as though the world and me were out of favour
And all I wanted to do was sit with my past and savour.

I am beginning now to see the difference in me,
And instead of asking you all, it's me who can see
See past the image I made in my mind
And look now to see if there are any true friends to find.

I am content to say that there still are.
Those true friends of mine who never go far.
I want to say to you all and please ignore my tear
And I am so glad, so happy that you are still here!

I urge you now to forgive my mistake
Look passed the unpleasant journeys my anger made us take
And please look to the future to the new happier side of me
I'm sure you will find that is someone you'd prefer to see!

Andy 24.06.97

To all those silently mentioned above. I hope that all is not lost!

My Vision

What will I be doing, one year from today?
Will I sit down in silence, or have yet more to say?
Will I even be here, alive or dead?
Having done all I could, having said all that's said?

To sit in the wee hours quietly thinking things through
Pondering the moment and all the things yet to do
I wonder sometimes if I'm what was meant
Writing down my words in solid cement.

When I look to a bright, sunny summers night
It fills me with words that I just have to write.
I do not see the surface of many a normal thing
I see an unwritten song that I just have to sing.

I sometimes wonder just what it would be like
To just sit and not think, to turn off my psyche.
Yet I have tuned it this way for so very long
That I just cannot ignore any kind of song.

I am like a human sponge, absorbing every word,
I know it sounds crazy, I know it's absurd,
And when I look at a wall, sometimes it's a fly
Other times it is sentiment, quietly passing me by.

It's not regret I feel, nor am I annoyed
That so little of my time can be deployed
To do what I want without the need to write,
Because never would I give up this special kind of sight

Andy 06.01.99

Neon Apps

Insidious, it has moved!
The beasts longer hide in televisions, on billboards
They are closer, closer
On my phone; in my apps!

Would you like a cookie?

It's not the cookie that I had in mind!
Now you will remember me... haunt me.
I turn you off, but you keep on plotting
Plan my screen for tomorrow! Hook; line; sinker!

And today's incredible offers pour forth!

How do you know I looked at that?
Yes do I need {Enter Product Here}
How do you know I needed that?
Oh yeah, I ate your damn cookie!

Unsubscribe?

Just another way to blind side me
Make-believe buttons to fool the stupid
Quixotic ideals - click to download
Look at me! I'm a war leader/soldier/piece of...

CAndy?

That's us all right.

Treats for the Neon
Swallow us whole, millions at a time
Install, fall, upgrade, persuade.

Data... Data....
Devourers of data
Down goes the intelligence, up goes the profit!
While we once again die a neon death!

But we try to... Try to ignore
And....
Oh wait!
Look!
Updates available!

Andy 10.11.15

No Other Way

After years of sitting in rooms trying to repent.
I no longer have a clue as to what they represent,
These feelings I have when the sunlight goes out,
These feelings of despair; of fear and of all out doubt.

When once I was so sure, so aware of my course
The times I spend yelling for help now have left me hoarse
And as I face another day full of uncertainty and concern
I must look to see if there's a different solution I must learn.

The pit of my stomach seems empty and hollow
With fears over the paths that I now must follow
For although I cannot see what will become of me,
I have no doubt that any joy that comes will not come free.

This is only the way that I feel today,
No doubt tomorrow will find me a different way.
But for now I hold back wondering what I will see
And then I must decide if that choice is the one for me.

Is there no other path, no other way I could possibly go?
No other choice that would help to hold back the flow?
I stand now once more, alone against the onslaught of rage,
Yet in the colourful history that is my life, this is but one single page.

Andy 28.04.97

Not Any More!

There's a line of division
That's setting between you and me.
There's a darker line, breaking apart
All the truths we built up over time.
And I can't tell if we're together any more!

Help me find the line we made,
I'd look myself, but I can't tell.
The truths and feelings are hidden
Below so many parodies.
And I don't know what's real any more!

You tell me that it's in my head.
But I wonder if that's another lie.
You try to break me, to take me apart
You look inside my mind and laugh.
And I don't want that any more!

People look at us and smile their smile.
As they think they know what they see.
Illusion creates its own sense of truth
And that's not always the proper one.
Though I can't tell the difference any more!

What's left then, to do?
Should I carry on, just pretending?
Pretending that the bricks and mortar are real?
More like paper in wind than anything else.
And I don't like it any more!

I can't take it any more!

Andy 09.10.97

Not You Again!

So you returned, back after so long.
To take from me joy, to rob me of song,
I thought the changed locks would keep you out for good.
But I guess I should of known that nothing ever could.

So what shall we do? Reminisce of old times?
Of how when I am with you the sun never shines.
Or when we sit together I would drink on my own
In my room by myself yet could still hear you moan.

So now we have taken our walk down memory lane.
I doubt that I could look back down again.
For I see the pain you have caused, all in my name
And all I can do is hang my head low in shame.

What prompted your return to the old ways?
Why come back now, today of all days?
I had just begun to feel my life was complete.
I see the fear and jealousy again begin to compete.

I guess I can't blame you, it just isn't right.
After all, it wasn't you who called for this fight.
Because if things were good, and path crystal clear
I wouldn't feel low, and you would not be here.

I will sit down and try to examine the cause.
To look for any gaps or for any obvious flaws,
They must be there, breaking holes in perfect life
Why else would I hold a bottle in one hand and in the other…

Andy 14.05.98 (Finished)

For that most silent of foes – the subconscious!

One Year Later

One year gone and things are still the same,
I'm still wondering who's at fault, where is the blame?
I still wear the same clothes; the same hair, the same smile
And I still drive the same damn road, mile after mile.

Again comes the letter inviting me to a gathering of friends
And again I'm still contemplating where to lay my bitter end,
The same type of phone call that spells out a different choice
If only I could pause and find my damn voice.

You haunt me now in my sleep, as I consider how you will look,
I am shaking in the dark as I try to escape your subtle hook
As you draw me closer with sheepish grin and gorgeous face
I will look back at my home, my chair, my kingdom; my place.

But for you I would gladly accept the judgement thrown my way
I am envisioning my defence and all the things I'll need to say
To justify the last six years of my life and all the pain that I've dealt,
But I can honestly say that with you I feel the things I've never, ever felt.

You make me feel the love of Life that I've failed of late to see,
You make me understand the stupid feelings that lie, buried deep within me,
I am not the sure footed mountain goat that once I assumed
But mere victim of the thoughts that leave me broken; consumed.

Where is the heart of your power over me? It's not in your mere appearance
That is just your face, merely the cause of the interference.
I am alive and this I never once paused or took time to consider,

And That little wisdom I don’t need an outside courier to deliver.

I will wait and see what develop this in this anticipated weekend,
In the few stolen hours that we together will spend.
I will take you as I find you, beautiful and willing to hear me speak,
And will lat last see if you truly are the freedom and salvation I so blindly seek!

Andy 07.12.04

Painter

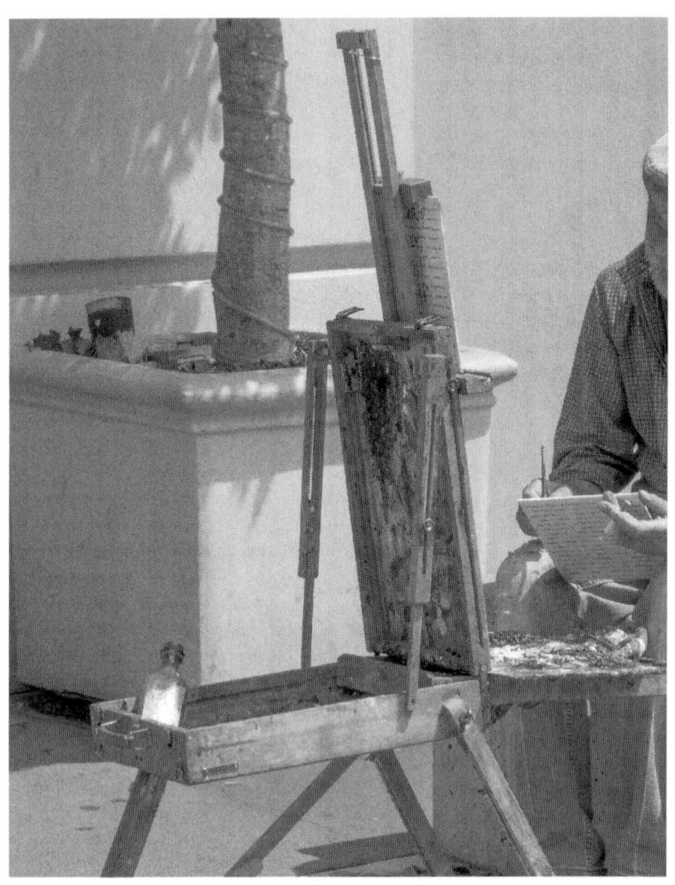

Painter

Every person paints a picture.
They are given the brush by their mother,
The canvas by father.
The paints from friends.

Now they must decide what to paint.
Should it be a painting to signify love?
Perhaps a rancid depicting of morality?
Or a canvas upon which even saints may weep.

They decides.
It takes a life to paint it,
And finally a soul to sell it.
When it's done, no prize awaits. Time to leave.

The critics study it. They decide if it is good.
If not they are shut down, no visitors, no credit.
In years to come we read about them, and the lonely quest,
Is just a figment remaining in an old tattered school book.

The black, say the critics, contrasts sharply with the red.
While the sharp undertones highlight the background.
Do they? Do they really? What kind of undertones do you mean?
Come to think of it, do you even see the meaning in the colour?

What kind of painting do they see with shallow eyes?
The work of a part-time person with a goal to become a painter?
The true meaning behind the meaning escapes
And instead they sip wine with his lordship and jury.

Lock the painter in a single room, no brush, no canvas.
To awake at night thinking of the paintings they could do.

They want to paint, can't you see that? But you wait for tomorrow,
With its onslaught of painters, they smile and don the wig!

Can you see it yet?
No? Look deeper.
No no! Much deeper than that!
It's there far behind the proverbial canvas...

Andy 21.01.95

Pause

Life doesn't matter at the end of the day
Cause all we have left is what we didn't get to say.
When you're lying in the dirt with friends saying "bye"
You find yourself looking at those who just don't cry.
Why, you ask yourself are they not feeling down?
As they lower the coffin, and you don't make a sound.
When all is said, and the eulogy is through
Do you spend some time just thinking what the hell to do.
As friends drop off, just disappear in the confusion
How long do you spend considering a conclusion?
While the bullets fly and people die, you pause and just think
On how much of life you left and how pungent was your stink?
Craters left to signify your blatant disregard
How many victims bear your wounding shard?
How often do to pause, just take a moment for prayer
And do you even see the people who pause and then stare?
When life turns round and suddenly you're in a war,
Do you look to the victims and wonder, what the fuck was it for?
Blue sky and green grass get charred in humanity's wake
Killing each other purely for killing's sake.
Sometimes I wish I could just blow this world to shit
Convinced by my mind, I wouldn't care one little bit.
So what am I trying desperately to say?
Nothing really, just the same shit I worry over every single day!

Andy 20.11.07 (Finished)

Reflecting Shadows

As I sit before the mirror, I notice the changes.
The changes in posture, in face, in eyes. In fact.
For my reflection is no longer my friend.
It sits, a challenger, an aggressor, an enemy!

There are times we meet a decisive fork in the road.
Person and shadow split, go separate ways, one left, one right.
Far down the road we look - no reflection. Who was right?
A frantic search uncovers cobwebs. Uncovers… nothing!

Years later the reflection returns
But he's not the same, he's bitter, he's hurt, he's broken!
To live without shadow is to lose the power of reason
No conscience remains to reflect upon, no sounding board for decision.

And so now we sit, my shadow and I, the two who were one.
Blinding realisation: We cannot stand each other.
A look of disgust as we see what each has become. The black, no white.
It's strange to see - these two moving together yet working alone.

No man should ever fight his own reflection
Of all things sacred your soul is your own.
Yet I fight with mine on everything, for nothing
I would smash the mirror yet the fragments would just laugh.

Far better the devil you know that the shattered pieces you cannot see!

Andy 20.04.99

Reflective Thoughts

I use these hands to write these words
I use this mind to think these thoughts,
I use this tongue to speak these lies,
I use this time to promise change.

What part of this do you believe?
What part of this makes you laugh?
What part of this makes you shake your head?
What part of this takes away your trust?

I try to convince myself that this all makes sense!
I try to convince you that I know what I'm doing.
I try to convince those people, who frown in my face,
I try to convince the world that I'm not truly insane.

I use my eyes to stare at the past.
I use these ears to hear what I want.
I use this dream to try and make sense,
I use this keyboard to write my apology.

When is the time to admit defeat?
When is the time to admit you were right?
When is the time to take a step behind?
When is the time to plan my escape route?

How was I to ever know?
How was I to ever get my chance?
How was I to ever walk away?
How was I to ever know my name?

Where were you when things went wrong?
Where was I when I should have understood?
Where was fate when my coin fell on its side?

Where was life when my last bottle fell flat?

What part of me went wrong?
I just never understood.
When time is fluid, and I stood still
How could I ever have known?

I have eyes,
I have reason
I have time
I have left it too late!

Andy 31.03.06

Replay

Plant your barbs when I don't hear
Then night comes, I feel, and I fear.
Seeds planted in the silence of the day
Return with a vengeance to vent, to torture, to replay.
Moments fragment, memories to analyse.
While deep inside it's me who slowly dies.

I rip and I tear, trying to make sense of what I feel
While more and more I begin to lose what is real.
Replay stolen moments I have no right to know
I wasn't there the first time, why book a seat at this show?
Yet I cannot forget, nor can I fully accept what's been before
So I forgo the moment, and all I have, in favour of sullied lore.

You come back again with that look that will ultimately forgive
Forget what has been, we are the ones who gets to live.
Yet synapses flash to give way to painful ideal
And no one can understand the agonies I inherently feel.
The past is still here it will never truly leave
It just moves away giving us more time to grieve.

And what now, is there a way to undo the damage I've seen?
Perhaps grow more memories, fill the spaces in between?
And if somehow I can forget all the atavistic lore I have been told
I might just be here in years for you to grab and hold.
Or maybe I'll drown in the quicksand of my own design
Still looking, still seeking for something; anything to call mine!

Andy 17.03.10

Reverie

Sleep. Once more
When it came
Was fleeting
Draining

Dreams once more evade
Stroboscopic images only
Serve as a denied reminder
Of a refreshed and perfect night
Amid warm duvet where
Maternal pillows protect
From the hunter-like beasts of the dark.

To awaken?

Why?

The day is formed and does not need me
I anoint myself to the lie. Let's do this!
Upon the youth-wasted young who scheme
It's my turn to promote rapacity
Why can't I cry?

I stepped out once
Embrace me!

Or deny me.
I don't mind
There's nothing they can do to me
That's not already been done.

Cruelty for cruelty's sake?

Evening assassins come with smiles
Why do they do that?

What are they waiting for - me to turn my back?
Bury your blade then. Do you mind if I don't smile?

Andy 21.08.20

Safari

I mentioned a while back, about splitting my soul
And told tales of how I could never again expect to be whole.
I explained how my choices in life have robbed me of joy
And left me now with the emotional age of a ten year old boy.

Though I was convinced that given time I could undo my mess,
Perhaps change where I was headed, or cover up and redress.
I thought my emotional state was just a storm I could bear
Come out the other side, and perhaps find myself there.

Then from out of the blue came a new and dangerous condition
Brought about by my lack of an informed or careful decision.
I thought where I was headed would bring about pastures new
And I was unprepared for when the god damned fuse blew!

To say I am worse off would be putting it too mildly
My life has gone mad so I panic and thrash about wildly,
Trying to make sense of the feelings that rip me apart from inside
Forcing me to turn away and pathetically try to hide.

My mind attacks me on a daily basis with crap I don't want to hear
Images flash; memories collide as I force back a tear.
I don't want to feel these things that I do I cannot take the pain
So I reach for the bottle and the knife all over again.

I am so deeply in love with a girl who will probably drive me mad
Yet she remains the best thing my insane life has ever had!
So why do I continue on this stupid safari of the mind?
I'm terrified of myself and worried over what I might find!

So again I go on and on about things I have no control over
A fact I find frustrating as I become less and less sober.
I had hoped to reverse my opinions on me, alter and revise
Yet I still remain the one person I truly, honestly, despise!

Andy 22.05.08

Shoulders

Could you remember me? Just not the way I am
A bitter, twisted and broken man.
Think of the way things used to be
When you held my heart and set me free.

Don't think of the ruined man with fear in his eyes
The one who used up all his tries
Think if you can, on times I called mine,
When the rain never fell and the sun did shine.

Face down in the gutter with life flying by
No one stopping to ask why I cry.
Fate's twist and life's joke is upon my shoulder
And my pain and fear never die, they just grow older.

Don't look at my ghost as it rattles its chains
Lamenting its loss and reeling from pains
In the end there was only one who held blame
And that was this idiot who thought to invent a new game.

My own mind continues to hide from reason
Instead seems hung up on continuing its journey into treason.
My bitter heart remains closed, my soul is forfeit
While once strong and secure sanity falters more than just a bit.

Remember me, of you can, or create a new lie
Something, anything that your broken soul could buy
When the dust settles and the agony subsides
Maybe we'll both understand if it's us or fate that ultimately decides.

Andy 26.10.09

Slam

Slam-punched another wall to make the anger go away
Didn't work
Now I've 14 guitars I'm unable to play.

I grabbed a knife to cut my skin, I don't care
Didn't work
Now I've clothes I can't even wear.

I yelled and screamed because I got angry on the drink
Didn't help
And I hurt those I love because... because I didn't think.

Didn't think of what it was I was doing to myself;
Didn't care
That it was ultimately costing me my health.

Slow burn suicide, on the way out
Why?
Even I don't know what that's all about.

Time to stop, to wake up and try life
Is there time?
Before I lose myself, my family; my wife.

No wonder you looked at me with that pained face
I'm sorry
You shouldn't have witnessed my damned disgrace.

Slam-punched another wall because the anger was in my way
Back again?
Back to the place where the demons come out to play.

Losing my life, and losing at life

All because the addictions of my demons
Are constant, and they are rife!

Andy 02.05.20

Slow And Absolute.

It's always there
In the back of my head.
There, in the corner.
On the answering machine.
In the inbox.

It's the reason.
The main reason.
You are not here.
I couldn't take the chance.
I couldn't make that call.

Selfish? Of course it is.
But somewhere along the way
I protected you.
Can you believe that?
I need you to believe that!

I almost called it today
I heard it... in the air.
A summer day blighted by storm,
A rainy day on a perfect picnic.
I waited on it calling today.

There it is! The reason you are not here.
The boss on my shield.
I am protecting you still
You must understand that.
I am protecting you... Still.

Because it's always there.
Always in my head.
My reasons; my excuses.

How can i pretend;?
How can I hide?
From my slow and absolute suicide?

Andy 12.12.15

I know the how and the where, it's the when that scares me

Sphere

I view the world these days through a lethargic grunt,
It appears I've lost the respect for life, I cannot hunt
Anymore for the things that once filled my breast
And now it robs me of smiles and leaves me distressed.
Where is my lust, where is my appetite, where is my goal?
Help me dammit! Has anyone seen my soul?

I see people so alive they make my head hurt
I can't get a taste of what they have; all I taste is the dirt
It fills my mouth as I fall to the ground
And as I make to scream no one turns round.
So I close my mouth and bow my head,
To sit in silence, alone instead.

So now I want to be alone with my near perfect sphere
Where I can't speak, can't feel and definitely can't hear
The others around me as they try to explain the love they feel
Yet they can't understand that their type of emotion can't always heal.
But still they try to penetrate my cloud of distress
They break in, hunt around, and look under the bed. God, what a mess!

Just leave me alone to contend with my self doubt
You couldn't comprehend or understand what it's really about
This fear I have that I will fall flat on my face,
With everyone around me to bear witness to my own disgrace.
So I want to hide, run deep into the trees, and run like the wind
So that I am truly alone, and no one will know that I tripped and I sinned!

Andy 21.06.01

Still The Natural Order of Things

A leaf blew and felled an empire.
Or so I thought
I lost more of me today.

Formless voids shape my evening dreams.

Solemn moments came again.
No longer fruitful, inaction has me rotten.
Choices considered, never planned. I am ill.

I cannot dream anymore?

What became of you?
Still here, but you vanished into what never was.
I hate who I have become.

Translucent futures, and thoughts are opaque
In these rewritten pasts of incorrect chapters and foolish grammar.

It's wrong.
It's still wrong.
And no one even sees.

Smile for the selfie
Record moments to fill with subversion.
Is there any truth in all this madness?

To them I offered devotion; to them I tried to feel love.
Yet I get nothing.
My knife did me harm, yet you cut me deeper.

I'm still on my own.

For an eon
And this is still the natural order of things.

Andy 25.04.20

Tangled

Who are you today?
Who am I?
Flick your switch.

Polarise me.
A turtle on it's back.
Sun baking – I cannot move.

Tunes in my head.
Aim to please
Pleas to aim.

Who knocks my door?
My head hurts... join the dots.
Knock, knock!

Who's there?
An ironic twist on a familiar take.

Can you loosen the thumb screws?
It hurts just a little too much today.

Rain in my face.

I slip in the dark.
I can't see my hand in front,
Or your hand behind.

Why?
It remains the question without answer.
A riddle, seemingly without end.

A rope has two ends. I think?

Yet mine has only one
Lost somewhere in the tangled mess.

Come to bed. Can you?
I don't want to talk anymore.
No more words. No more thoughts.

Please, god. No more wars.

Andy 20.04.10

The Agonies of Yesteryear

Why is it that every time I speak?
You look at me as though you want to weep?
I have really done so very, very wrong,
This devil with pointed tail and prong?

Why is it that you cannot hear?
My every word falling upon a deaf ear?
I try my very best to make you understand,
As my mind wanders to its far off land.

The words I speak are not so vile,
Yet you walk away mile after mile.
I shout above the crowd for you to hear.
Yet I anger and hurt you year after year.

Am I to blame for this downright lie?
I am forced to cower away, so very, very shy
As I look at the past with all of its pain
I cry at last as I see it was all in vain!

I love you more than anyone, don't you know?
As the months pass by it becomes harder to show
Still I want to embrace you and scream out loud
"I love you!" Yet I am a fool who is just too proud.

A man's foolish pride causes him to sit alone,
The love he feels has passed away, I hear me moan
I had a chance to do things right and with pride
But the recent memory is like a knife deep in my side.

Give me another chance; let me prove my right
Your recent vows caused me to cower, recoil in fright
As I saw the hurt, pain, anger, rage and fear

That becomes my epitaph every single, lonely year!

Andy 02.06.94

The Big Fight

As the surrounding lights dim
And the spotlight shines.
The crowds cheer
As the fighters enter.

The stances are adopted.
I see the gowns fall off,
The referee strikes the bell
And the first vocal punch is thrown.

The Champ recoils, hit by the force.
The acid stain draws yells from the crowd.
He stumbles, stunned by the first round.
The Challenger smiles. A smile of salty tears.

The Champ stands again, excitement mounting.
He fires a quick left outspoken jab.
The Challenger recoils, fires back
And I watch, with heavy heart, the constant fight.

I see the fighters sit and watch
Each other, with a glimmer of tomorrow's hope.
I wait with bated breath for round two.
Will it happen? Round two? I pray and wait.

The referee smiles, strikes the bell.
The fighters rise, once more ready for battle.
Voicefull gloves at the ready. Charge!
I turn away, soul-sickened and cry in the ring.

Andy 08.07.95

The Bitter Memory

You were there for me in a time when I was weak
When simple solutions to problems I would blindly seek.
There you stood, a simple smile reaching out to me
The wink of an eye suggests how things could be.

I talked with the hint of fire in my voice
That backed you off, left you no choice
But to hang up with anger and a hint of pain
That will leave me in the morn with more than shame.

Turning blindly, I reach out with fear entwined
I blast the clock and its inability to unwind.
Or to pass through the choices made in haste
And so curse its omissions that I was unable to taste.

The master holds his key in check
And honours the demons who steal and wreck
The haunted images it cannot tolerate or view
You curse me and so in turn I curse you too!

Pull me back with talk of a better time,
The images you speak of begin to unwind
Until I cannot see passed my own fear or memory
And Past it grips, takes control of the little that is left of the Me.

I say to you, with tears in our four eyes
Don't cry for me, no matter how our truth lies.
For never once was I able to see the thread upon the loom
And therefore I stand a lone with my God and face my doom!

Andy 09.01.98

Dedicated "fondly" to the hour of three am. That little hour that hands you all problems on a plate!!

The Blend Lead

The words don't come any more, nothing, nothing...
My mind, once fall of interpretation remains silent.
A tree is just a tree and there is only one meaning now,
No longer multiple answers to multiple questions.
All but one track is gone from me now and it's the one I fear.
Normality. Humanity. Blind sheep herding together to... where?
I find myself locked onto the path I went to extremes to avoid.
Fallen finally deep into the abyss. How much memory remains?
How long until I no longer can look back up the path I came?
How long until the crossroads I feared so much slips away?
The sacrifices I made in order to record my fears seem futile.
No longer a taste for the meal I worked so hard and so long to prepare.

I have different eyes now than twelve years ago, choices I made seem stupid.
I see the boy I was, who thought he knew where to go, yet maturity changes,
And instead I see the blindness I called vision that sent me stumbling.
What was I thinking? What were you thinking? There he goes, fucking up again!
One wish remains now. The wish to see the crossroads again, to avoid the abyss.
The one place I was sure I would never see becomes instead my only home.

What am I saying with these, my foolish words? Like always I really don't know. Would my desire to avoid the abyss really be my salvation? Is there another?
What if, perchance, I embraced the abyss from an early age?
Became as you?

In the kingdom of the blind the one eyed man is king! Maybe, but then again
The one eyed man is still not without his faults. He carries the prejudice of anger And perhaps after all that I've said these past twelve years, it's my sin as well!
I find myself beginning to look forward to life inside the sphere of humanity.
I find I no longer have to see things in stereoscopic sight, I have found the mono.
The place where my friends live, where my family live where everyone lives,
And after all this time I find there is no longer a sickening fear at becoming so,
I read the daily papers, I drive slowly to work, I wonder at normal things. But!
It's the night I fear! The barriers drop, the mind's eye opens and I again become me!

Andy 19.02.03

The Colour Red

The solemn bell strikes.
An unwelcoming, unnerving clang that shakes the very fabric of night
A tear, perhaps unnoticed, forms anew to seek comfort in the pillow's depth.
Why is the sunset to be red once again?

A wound is born
Made manifest in the cooing gurgle of a newborn
People rush past, they do not see
That my blood is just as red.

I think too much in the cold of evening's rain
Thoughts that do not become me.
I have no conscience toward tomorrow.
Why should I when warm waters run red?

There is always next time, goes the condolence
Ad infinitum and results remain unchanged.
"Look on the plus side", the irony is too much to bear.
To one who has seen enough red tides to last a life time!

Andy 12.08.11

The Darker Side

As I look at our world, spread green and lush below.
I see a darker side, like a volcano, ready to blow.
For amid the paradise with flowers so green
Lie the remnants of war that shatter man's dream.

The truth of war and all it represents
Hides all man's lies, his truths and his repents,
For one man's ideas, another must pay
Soldiers listen to the majors and all that they say.

The casual man who fights in the trench
Is the only one who sees, who smells the stench
Of ruined bodies as they lie in shallow grave
Oblivious now to all they tried to save.

Oh poor victim of war and belief
Love ones remain, no one hears their grief
As they pray and shout to the ones who do not hear
Nor do they see the silent fall of the crystal tear.

Tyrants alone, who think they know it all,
Who think they themselves can answer the call
So with a quest in their hearts they try to save man’s dream
Pity them, for they cannot see that all is not what it seems.

Andy 02.07.97

The Frog And The Dog

I am tired.
Too tired. To talk.
I have not even the strength
To fight the TV, let alone me.
Air hangs like a heavy curtain
From which even light cannot see

Forty six years of fighting this system
Only to find out everyone is blind, deaf, and dumb
Plans I had made and tried to set in motion
Fell apart between promotion and demotion
You bet I am tired and sick of this game
I want to run away, but they chained me; made me lame.

Smile as the man throws a bone from his table
That's ok when I was young, fit, and able
Now I am older with teeth worn from chewing that bone
And as I look for help from others I find I am still alone.

As I stand knee deep in a pile of shit
All my work and worry doesn't matter one tiny bit
For as I struggle to throw it all over the place
There is always some bastard throwing more in my face.

I'm finished, I'm done, fed up being a working dog
Have I finally, finally understood the axiom of that boiling frog?

Andy 17.06.20

The Enemy

What the hell is wrong with me?
Searching, always searching
For a new way to kill me.
The enemy within?

It was always me.
Do you see?
The enemy
Was always me.

Assassination plots
Foremost in my mind
One day I'll find
The bullet meant for me.

Bang!

Act surprised, sunshine,
The people demand a scene
Scripted theatrics
Maybe just a little obscene?

Perhaps it's time.
Let hope die
Let them cry
Let me wonder why

In the end what truly is worse?
To live with false hope
Or to believe there is hope?
Who can tell.

Give me fifteen minutes

In that other place.
Damn the cost
I've paid more for less!

Watch me become egregious
While I try to assume the norm
Something not right In the trying
Or maybe it's all on me.

Do you see my enemy?

Andy 21.08.20 (Finished)

The Hole In My Chair

Turn that mirror away. I can't face what it shows!
I already looked inside and administered the blows.
What could it show that I don't already know?
Just some ignorant idiot hung up on being low.

Turn it away I said! I can still see my own face!
Sitting down in silence in my sickly, solemn place.
Reflecting now on choices made that I couldn't understand
I didn't see the cards being dealt and couldn't play my hand.

What's that in the mirror? A stupid scowling frown!
Looking on in wonder at the dour-faced lonely clown.
He stares at the world through painful gritted teeth
And all because I cannot face what lies underneath!

I sit on my chair and look at the hole my arse has worn
All because it's the only place I can wait and truly mourn
How many times will I dance to a tune only I can hear?
How many times will I wait for you to come and wipe my tear?

If only I never had to look at my face again! Would that help at all?
Would it keep me from sinking down, and stop the painful fall?
This moment of madness that rises from my insane plan!
The moment in life that makes me think: "I'm fucking superman!"

So take the mirror from my hands, and let me think instead
Just consider all the things I've done, the stupid things I've said
Why do I always end up doing the same thing?
To sit alone at the end of the day picking at the sting!

Andy 07.08.07

The Junkie Who Lied

For the want of a few thousand pounds I can't be who want
So I use what I have to tease and to taunt
I sniff and I rub into gums become numb
To devour what I have and then some.

Try to sleep in the midst of a high
Toss and turn, shake, and then sigh
Then awake with a start when sunlight pours in
Disgusted at my outside and what's become of within.

All that I am is mere illusion laid bare
By the cold, sad soul who was never really there.
I can't sing that song; I can't write that last lyric
I can't admit the truth - that my fight is now pyrrhic.

I used to be alive, deep on the inside
Now I find only the junkie who lied
This is the last, tomorrow I'll quit
Ashamed that I even believed my own shit.

And what of you when you see the truth
When my lies are exposed as painfully uncouth?
Will you still want to stay, even for a while?
Could you still walk toward me down that aisle?

How many will stand in shock when they see
The horrific exposé that is the real me?
I am not who I claimed, nor who I said
I try to be alive when I'm already dead.

Words I proffer up in cryptic lines are misunderstood
They say instead the things I never could
On the outside I smile and I look like I'm fine

Deep inside this cancer I create is anything but benign.

I died again in a room full of friends
I played my parts to their painful bitter ends
A preplanned piece to convince and to deceive
While the real me yelled and begged for you to leave.

Andy 31.03.02

The Man

On the ground lies a man.
Not a hero, or God. Just a man.
His face tells of lies and pain,
But look, in his eyes is a hope.

The business suit he wears is worn now,
The seams torn, the lapel creased.
His briefcase, full of wonders and promises,
Holds nothing but empty air now.

The suits and ties walk past him in the snow.
He is of no more importance now, why care?
His eyes open sadly, a look of hope passes,
But is quickly lost in the sneer of a stranger.

The hopeless eyes follow the stranger.
He looks at the suit, the neat seams, the tidy lapel.
He stares at the briefcase, sees the tight hold there.
The man sighs, and follows the future with his stare.

In the morning light the snow lies all around,
The promise of today arrives with the sun.
The today people walk around with hope, look down and frown.
And wonder who would leave such a nice briefcase in the snow.

Andy 25.03.95

The Memory Will Do

When you requested that last song
When you realised you stayed too long
When they no longer come to that birthday surprise
When you realised they believed those last few lies.

What happens then?

When the truth leaves you with nothing to defend
When all the promises have reached a natural dead end
When you can't tell enemy from friend
When you realise there is no one on whom you can fully depend.

What happens then?

Role model?
Reviled villain
Dunno, just some guy
No one!

I know the sadness in the truth:
I'll burn up long before I can be of real use - To you.
The memory will have to do
Perhaps, someday, I'll be overwritten.

In the end,
It doesn't matter

I wanted what killed me
I reviled what could save me.
I burned before I died.
I spoke truth when I should've lied.

And I never got to thank you for the flames.

I’m sure that the memory will do.
Once we assign names to the blames
You know I understand, and I’m sure you do too.

Andy 22.06.18

The Real World

Who determines the real world? Who makes the rules?
Who are really the smart ones, and who are really the fools?
Some people are born into money, they inherit the greed
And there are others who live never getting what they need.

I spent a long time resenting my parents because I wanted money,
Looking back at my anger I find so much that was funny.
You see I wanted to be rich, to have the most expensive toy,
And to this day, I'm running around still that stupid little boy.

Why are some people just given all at birth and never want?
Then waste what they have, searching for ghosts to haunt?
Denied the journey that comes with fighting for what you got
Until in the end they hate themselves, and end up losing the lot.

I fight for each and every inch of space, a war without end,
Because in the end I have nothing else, no one on whom to depend.
No summer mansion, complicated wine cellar, no private jet or gold
But when it all comes down to it, I have so much more that I can hold.

I have what these millionaires crave in their lonely, suspicious life,
I have my family, my car, my own home and a beautiful wife.
Yet I cannot help but feel envy when I see these millionaires,
And at the same time hating God for never answering my prayers.

I just want to be rich; to not worry about my endless bills,

But instead I want to devote myself to discovering new daily thrills.
I want a sports car, and a huge villa in the sun
Because only then, will I be able to feel like I've truly won!

I'm bored with living in this working class place
I want to be a super star, with people admiring my disgrace,
Throw TV's from hotels, take baths in champagne, and forget the real world.
I just want to launch my private yacht, get those sails unfurled!

Andy 16.01.06

The Wake Up

As my morning broke, something stirred.
I awoke.
For the first time in years I grew aware of life.
I opened my eyes
saw a world of wonder I had long abandoned
I took a breath
Felt the fire explode deep in my chest.

What ended this self imposed coma?
What brought me from years in the dark
Why now can I again taste fruitful life?
The reason is clear, You!
From the wreckage I called my life
You appeared, breathing life into my bitter remains
And tore from me the sleep of a hundred years!

So now I'm awake what happens next?
Images flash, hopes rise, emotions fall
All in a heartbeat, in a single gasp.
I struggle to maintain order in chaos
I've slept for a life time; now I am addicted to life.
Yet the moment you withdraw I'm lost again
Eyes close, breath fails and my fragile candle winks out.

So will you keep me from perpetual sleep?
Will you breath vital life into a burning ember?
I have but a flicker of hope in the encroaching dark,
One small vision of a life that could be, should be!
With what strength remains me I offer you my hand.
My eyes have closed in fear as I fearfully await my fate.
Will your hand take mine, or will I again slip and succumb to sleep

Andy 19.09.07

Maggie....

There Came A Day…

There came a day and I was born.
The nurses smiled, the doctors went on a break,
My dad got drunk and my mum cried.
My grandparents beamed with beatific smiles
Then when my eyes opened, the world appeared
It said hello, then challenged me. Can you do better?

I went to school to learn the way of things,
English, maths, physics, history and wood work.
I was told to become an amalgamation of those things
Write down what they tell you, study it all, then… unlearn.
It's called your formative years, yet I always thought that wrong,
Truth has made me realise that instead, we should call it fermentation.

My life has always been like a cheap flat packed do-it-yourself wardrobe
It ends up looking nothing like the box; instructions missing.
I tried my best to fit the pieces together, sometimes shaving the ends,
But it was only to make them fit, and not to cheat.
Am I missing more than the instruction manual? Am I missing the point?
Maybe the joy is in the building and not in the finished product?

It's amazing, this thing we all call life! Nothing ever repeated!
We might moan and complain, that we're living the same each day,
But think, really think, when will today ever come again?
How much have we left unfinished today, into bed and not a care,
Trusting in whatever God we pray to, that we can finish it tomorrow!

We are thrust into this world with odds that no self-respecting bookie would trust
Yet there are those among us that can clean out the house!

Andy (Finished) 26.10.05

This Crazy Scenario

As I turn around, to look within my mind
I see the edges of my sanity begin to fray and unwind.
At present the clear has disappeared to be replaced with mud
And the ties are now water when once they were blood.

Nothing can be made of this change in Today,
There is nothing I can think of and there is nothing to say
I will have to sit in silence and wait for the melt
That comes with the realisation of the guilt we felt.

When I look to see where the blame will lie
I don't know if there is a clear path to try
No way to see what caused this crazy rift
So, on our knees, deep in dirt, we begin to sift.

I hope that tomorrow we can stop this insane fight
And come together in hug with faces shiny, happy and bright.
Until then we shall pass each other with stares in the hall
And ignore the love in our hearts that won't stop its frenzied call.

Andy 18.08.97

To Change

Ah so today I am the Loved.
Yesterday I was the Bad.
What lies for tomorrow?
The Bastard, the Hero, the Worshipped?
Tell me please.

Why must I be these different people,
In your eyes?
Can't you be content,
With one alone?
Spin the wheel, choose my role.

Why must one see white
The other black?
Paths never cross between the pair
Oppose each other, be content
With making me the scapegoat.

And so tomorrow arrives.
Choose... who am I today?
I must ask
The Lover, the Loved?
The Hater the Hated?

Or perhaps a new role.
For me to play today.
The Outsider, the Heretic?
The list is endless, Oh Ruler,
The list is endless...

Andy 27.04.93

Too Bitter A Pill

These days I feel drained, with the world on my shoulders
And more and more, I feel it's made up of giant boulders.
I don't know how long I can play this wretched old game
The pieces don't move and the board always looks the same
And I doubt if I'd throw the numbers I need on the old tattered dice
And doubtless anyway, that I could afford their bitter price.

I am pulled in so many directions all at once, where am I?
No matter how I hold on they always manage to pry,
They take my strength, my vision, then pull it all, what a mess
And I am stuck on this board in a game of life long chess,
Take only what you need, don't empty me out,
Yet you don't understand, just tell me "Shh! Don't shout".

I can lie in a corner, drained of all that I am,
I put on a face, you smile, God what a sham!
Little wonder, then you can't see me any more
And pass by my soul that's spilled on the floor.
I try to be what you all want me to be, no matter the occasion
And again I succumb to your bitter pill of persuasion.

Oblivious it seems, to my unique point of view
I try to tell you my side, yet you just run me through.
Don't pull me apart any more, I don't have anything to give
You've drained me of all, left only with the will to live,
Even that, you work on, sculpting 'til it fits what you decree,
Until it becomes a better vision, minus all I had of Me.

I swore last time, I would never again go your path,
Turning I see I have, and now understand that bitter last laugh.
The path I thought I had dug with my own broken hands
Was never mine, cause underneath your one still stands.

"It's for you own good," can't have you making this great
mistake"
Well, dammit at least it was mine, and that you can't ever take!

Andy 09.01.99

Unbreakable

I always thought, well, until today really
That suicide was quick and instant.
I never considered that it can take years.
Never thought that I was already on my way there.

Even now, with the acid sting of sudden realisation
Burning in my head, I'll still on track.
Still dying of a thousand cuts, both physical and metaphor.
Pieces fall away, some painfully slow, others in a heartbeat.

Take yesterday for example. No blood, but a cut none the less.
This time: my father. He fell from me with angry, bitter tears.
In the same instant I realised how truly alone I really am now.
Even my shadow turns the other way. No one understands.

So how far through my life-long suicide am I now?
How long have I still to go? I wonder what cuts I'll make next.
Who will fall victim to my insecurities; to the demonic voice only I hear?
I belittle what I've done, crave what I don't have, all the while yearning for peace!

I have, in this last year, impacted my life with the force of an atomic bomb.
I have obliterated every single fragment and every single piece.
Nothing was safe!
Not one thing remains the same; I have become almost the negative image of myself.
Yet even here, now, I cannot stand myself. No matter where I go, there I am!

I can't stand it! Can't stand being with me constantly.
If only I could fall apart as easily as everything else.

All around me I create chaos and devastation, ruining everything I have,
While standing like some immortal goddamn unbreakable clown who just won't die!

Andy 19.06.08

Fear is a powerful enemy, and I don't even remember now who I was when I wrote this - it's proof positive that even in the darkest times, light will come. (And "obliterating my life" was still the best decision I ever made).

I've included this poem in the hope that it might help even one person realise that the dark time won't last.

Andy 2020

Violence of Nightmares

I am dying right here.
I can already feel the fear.
Prophecies that were thrown in my name,
All the visions that ended in my solemn shame,
They are almost upon me now
And ironically I no longer need to ask "how?"
Warnings and gut feelings prove themselves real
As more and more I find myself hurting at how I feel.

Violence of nightmares cast shadows over all events
Ghostly images and apparitions appear, offering their
represents.
Tearful moments and furtive glances are all that remain
Of once proud and happy times now blackened by stain.
Time moves forward, never slowing or pausing in its track
I halt momentarily to remove the knives buried deep in my
back.
A shallow, quick breath as comprehension reveals its true
design:
The paradoxical fact that life was never truly mine.

Whispered words made out to me evade my understanding
A skydiver in freefall now terrified of the impending landing.
It's all come undone, to be splattered all over my landscape
Solid memory and safe conclusions fall victim to violent rape.
Tensions mount, thoughts are struck, watch the unbreakable
break.

I am forced into compromise; forced to lose more as again I forsake.
Fragments of moments, flashes of painstakingly manufactured promises all collide
Don't you see though, I take it all, the pain, the shame, the rage to remain by your side.

Andy 11.01.10 (Finished)

Watching God

I bear witness today to a new kind of God,
He stands above and watches; a law unto himself.
He has the power to take the power that gives
He holds all life in his hands yet cares not.

No compassion has this god, he just watches.
He stares with a Hippocratic eye, never feeling or loving.
To such a one we are numbers. Step back file 365
And keep off the grass!

His metal eyes swivel and watch as we go.
He calls to a friend to watch where he cannot
Down the line we go to another, another. Watch out he's leaving!
Don't worry; we have him in our sights. Click! Thus one's ours!

The accused cannot hide, he has been seen, been stamped.
A file has his name now; it lurks in silence, growing, a quiet witness.
The judges call their gods who in turn call their minions.
Observe! Our names become numbers our lives a file. We are lost!

To hide becomes a dream, a tale to tell children.
But speak it quietly; take care, for they watch from the skies
Filling up their files with data and with numbers.
We are seen. We are caught. We are punished. We are gone!

Those who pass through are but overflowed files.
Their names somewhere, lost in a surge of numbers.
Don't worry though, we can keep constant track,
Because the Gods above know where we are. Always.

They watch…

Watch…
Watch….
And watch…

Andy 14.01.99

What Am I?

I am the hurricane that yearns for release, yet remains kept in the jar.
I am the tectonic plate that shifts in solitude against the planetary axis.
A boiling nexus point that fears the multitude; that exacerbating, unconsciously malevolent force that moves as one. Unaware of its neighbour or of its destination.

Who can I be?

But the one who was made. Forged in the flames by the strike of the madman's hammer Who knew not what to create. Solemn statues that speak in silence and rage on berating the very instrument they adore. Watch carefully as the metal cools. See the shock as the once fluid creation settles into its unbending and unending shape.

Why?

Why not? Would be a better question; more possible answers to satiate the perverted. Indignant dreams that tear sleep from its deepest parts are not always welcome in the dead of night. Epiphanies sold by the dozen, I laugh at the wide eyed as they slam head first into their moment of revelation, realising too late that what was behind was not the loathsome tragedy that they thought. The future can be a cruel gift.

Can I?

Of course you can! Were you not bred thus? To see the paths in the choosing and not the choosing in the paths; is that not the ultimate gift of our species? The brain is not vestigial despite mans attempt to try. Using instead a well versed safety net that ensures infinite variables are reduced to one word: Fate. Ahh, but that is too easy. To own the choice means to own the blame!

I didn't want!

Want to what? To be, to think, to know? These are the cruel facts of our existence. We make our own rules and we make our own gods just so that they can take the blame for us and absolve us of guilt. "It was God's will" Ha! I laugh at the idiom as I laugh at you! Nothing is more terrifying than the knowledge that nothing is permanent and nothing lasts forever, everything is transitory. There is the real reason for ecclesiastical need.

We are who we are meant to be: the ultimate creators of chaos, oxymoronic in our origin and parsimonious with our genius. Dumb persistence over abstract choice, what chance did we ever have as our lethargy and herd-like mentality drive our species towards its pre-planned annihilation and a soothing, welcoming oblivion that we have populated with paradisiacal and paradoxical myth. We are not what was intended.

Andy 28.08.11 (Finished)

What The Hell

What the hell is wrong with me?
I cannot think, let alone see.
I'm so confused, my head is stress
My whole damn life is mad, and all a mess.

What the hell has brought me to this?
Once was calm, sedate, full of bliss.
Words appear on this stupid computer screen
And I spend hours wondering what they mean.

What the hell am I doing now?
Sitting in silence, wiping my brow.
Watching over my shoulder, afraid to look,
Afraid to see what part of my life you just took.

What the hell would I be able to say?
If this all came out at the end of the day.
Would people be shocked, look at me in disgust,
Even after all the lies had faded to dust.

What the hell is making me do this?
I am intrigued, yet powerless to resist.
Even as I walk, to check the computer screen,
I am left feeling angry, and I feel completely obscene.

What the hell brought me to this place,
An area full of danger and of all out disgrace?
I act the fool, more and more each day
As I spit-type words, adding yet more to this play.

What the hell would the other people do?
Where would we be, once their anger was through?
Would we be left alone, outcast and lost?

Overawed and overwrought at the ultimately human cost?

What the hell can I do?
But hang on in there, see this thing through.
I have no idea of where it will lead,
And of how much blood I'll be forced to bleed.

Andy 04.10.06

What the hell am I really doing?

What? Why? How?

What have I done?
Delusions of grandeur filled my head,
Dragged down deeper into enemy waters instead.
Lost within the deep, the dark, the completely wrong,
I was forced to walk a road to winding, so bleak, so long.
What did you say?
Things to make me look up from the shit I'm in.
Telling me, "don't worry, kid. This time you can win!"
Closer inspection makes me realise you don't have a clue
So in the end it comes down to an arena between me and you.
Why did you say it?
Why make me promises that you were unable (unwilling) to keep?
Make false idols to gods that don't exist, make sinners weep?
I stood at the crossroads, the abyss leering again from inside my mind
I looked at your offer of security, at the breadcrumbs you left lying to find.
Why did I listen?
To the inane promises you made, call me "son", take me under your wing
Tell me? Would you have waited 'til I was trapped before showing the bee sting?
How long would I have to wait, lying content at last in my bed
How long would it take before you pulled back the dream to reveal the deadly web?
How could I?
Ever have believed that there was a shining light above the dark?
How could I have failed to see your agenda; the fact you're the shark!
The big fish in the little pond? Ha! Had I listened to your bullshit, you're bait.

I'd have been the catch of the day, little more than a victim of fate!
What can I do?
To screw up the chances given me during the birth canal,
I have forfeited the great, the something and substituted the banal.
Little more than a scared child, dressed today in daddy's suit,
Place my ass on the line, and quietly await the drill sergeant's boot!

Andy 03.06.02

Little doubt that I shall remember this mistake

When Dreams Lie

Today I am sat upon my lonely old throne
Surrounded by toys and all I have known.
They lie scattered below testaments to all that I am
Yet the question remains, are they real or sham?

I can look at what's done with a regretful stare
And can offer free advice - watch out and beware,
Don't narrow your vision to one single aim
You'll only get lost searching out what's to blame.

I am living now off old glories and occasions
Avoiding more and more my self-made deliberations
My thoughts these days are focused more on what's gone
And even there I find I can't quite stomach my song.

Regrets are dead weights that drag you to ground
And blame is the carousel spinning you round and round
Fall under these devils and you lose yourself
To find your dreams rotting on a broken shelf.

Watch out for your dreams, don't let them take hold
Keep them close and treasure them like gold.
They are a luxury to look at and should not be out their place
For that's then they turn and slap you hard in your face!

Andy 24.11.98

Where Are You?

Where are you? They're waiting.
Tables are set, adorned with gifts,
They sit with bated breath, staring ever upwards,
Waiting for a sign, a fanfare to signal you are on your way.
Yet the skies remain clear, the path to the door silent.
Curtains are opened, peeking for a sign, yet, you have not come

A heavy sigh signifies another restless night.
You did not come. The table remains untouched.
Pillow absorbs yet another night of endless tears.
A hand is placed, full of hope and prayer, it remains…warm.
Will they open their eyes; risk a look to face another blank?
Dawn cries its solemn arrival, still you have not come.

Prayers go unanswered, there is no knocking door.
There is but a little hope left in the well. Another month
unfruited.
The field is planted with prayers and yearning…
Eyes meet, ever hopeful, yet are dashed upon the solemn red
wall.
Dreams turn ever inwards, haunting in their melodies.
And still, you do not come.

They seek answers from charts, from figures, from suited
clowns.
All scratch whatever head they have, blindly offering guesses.
The blame is cast in multiple directions, to be batted away.
Each night they close the curtains; turn off the light.
And turn to each other, grasping what little straws remain.
And in the cool morning light … you still have not come.

But they will wait. Indefinitely wait.
We smile, we hope, we will pray, and we will try.

We have the warmth of each other, the trust and the love.
Memories of old and prayers of the future we have in excess.
We still set the stage, and recite the words and plan the moment
For when the curtains open, and you really have come!

Andy 07.11.06

It was never me - I can, however, appreciate the sentiment.

Whisper of Thought

What has happened? Where are my dreams,
They lie broken and torn, just shadows on the floor.
The wind blows and rattles their ghostly chains,
Like some undead creature they stir and they moan,
Yet the wind dies and again they fall. Lifeless. Dead.

Once upon a time I was a cup overflowed.
Too many dreams, too little time. What to do?
Each day was a dream state, I could not fit them all.
Today I sit so tired. Shattered dreams upon the floor, silence behind.
I am like a fish yearning sea, only to discover he can't swim.

I look at my hands, what are they?
I once thought them creative, a craftsman's
Looking how I see only a lump of flesh
With marks where the nails have bitten.
Better to tear them off, than live yet one more lie.

How many lies have passed me today?
How many have I lived though choice, through no choice?
Creating images, flash goes the mirror and I saw a fool!
Yes, a fool surrounded by his fool's gold.
Laugh Midas, you old goat. I understand your game!

I parade around, a new toy, a new dream.
See mommy, I'm a rock star today!
You look with that look and nod your acceptance.
I pull away, and strum my tunes. What's wrong?
Why do you laugh? Don't you like my new emperor's clothes?

I played myself from so many stages. A puppet.
Pull my strings. Left and I grin, right and I frown.

Dress me as you will, how do you want me today?
I'll play for you, no problem, just don't leave me.
When you're gone I lie broken, batteries not included.

I watch again as another idea goes up in flames.
Ashes, ashes upon the floor. A wind and they're gone!
I sit again, looking for something new, yet finding nothing.
All around the sickening taste of old, of familiar.
I am played out, nothing else to bleed. I am silenced.

Just a whisper of a thought.

Andy 03.03.99

Whispering Dawn

At the edge
Something
Outside the door
Someone
Inside my head
Something.
Someone.

In the dark
A whisper
In the dawn
A cry.
Inside my head
A whisper
A cry.

A flutter of lips
They promise
A touch of hands
A lie.
Inside my head.
They promise.
A lie.

Can't live outside
Can't live inside.
Can't love outside
Can't love inside.

Something
In the dawn
Promises

Something
In the dark
Lies.

Where
In all of this
Am I?

Andy 30.03.16

Whisperings

Would you split me once more
Into yet even smaller pieces?
How many pieces will truly satisfy your demands?
You tear me apart 'til what's left will be no use to any one.

It's gotten to the point I can't tell any more.
Can't tell what is the true picture.
Faces under cloak and dagger whisper in secrecy,
Editing the information that I am finally given.

Damn you all!
Damn it all to hell, I just don't want to know anymore!
It's past the point now where I really care.
Just carry on whispering, juggling your truths.

This anger I have won't last for long.
There will come a time where I must forfeit.
A time when I must accept your way of life,
But ask yourself - is it really the fair way to go?

What about me? Can't I have a say?
You talk and you talk, all about me, making paths.
Leave it alone, dammit! let me make my own way.
For God's sake at least let me be my own man!

But I know that will never happen.
The whisperings are what really matter to you.
Not me, the fleshy undertones; the character in your plays.
Well now it's my turn to talk so just get the hell out of my life!

Andy 18.11.96

White Blanket

Isn't it funny, how a single, weary man
Spends his whole life building a pedestal?
He climbs to the top, exhausted, to look around,
And, caught by a wind, he falls to the bottom.

The bruised man is faced with a choice:
Should he climb once more? Or walk away?
But a lifetime spent building, he thinks,
Paves the way for a future in dust!

Is there someone up there, watching him?
Someone who controls the vicious wind?
He sees the man build with pride and love.
He laughs and laughs and turns on the wind.

The man tries once more, to climb.
This time he ties a rope to the top.
The wind blows, he stays on, firmly.
Is it all you dreamed of, man?

The feeling of joy is gone as he surveys his land.
All he feels, in the pit of his belly, is emptiness,
A life given to his work is spread before him.
Yet all he sees is an empty sheet - his own.

He looks to the sky and cries out loud!
Where are the rewards for his efforts?
A scorned loved one, a lost friend
And, above all...nothing...

Andy 14.12.94

Who Shaping Who?

I heard a saying once "The day the flesh shapes and the flesh the day shapes!"
At the time I considered it the most profound statement I had ever heard.
Later as I realised my place in this life, I was able to understand fully.
I am what they call "The flesh the day shapes".

Can you comprehend the true meaning behind that statement?
Empty minds struggle on in a vague attempt at comprehension.
I open my eyes each day and silently await the suggestion.
The sealed orders in brown envelope that dictate my response.

Some people are born with the ability to manipulate the grammar,
That is to say, that they can form their question, instigate a course of play
Others, like me, are forced instead to formulate a response!
Understanding, it seems, is based solely on the cells point of view!

Take today as an example, look to the trials forced upon me!
Some madman in front, a wooden desk between me and hospitalisation,
What defined this crucial moment? My nerves, my bravado, my engrams?
We come once again to the question: who shall shape who in this daily game?

Were I born with provocation rather than with question, I might have stood a chance;
been able to reply with instinct, rather than behavioural sense.

In the end who's to judge? Defined by genes, not by intimidation
and so I succumbed.
Some fools ability to exert far exceeded mine, so I fell, a victim
of cliché, not of truth!

We are born with a sense of right versus wrong, implanted with
our genes,
It's only when we're educated that we begin to falter; to question
our very cells.
Things that are solved with ease in the animal kingdom make no
sense to our intellect,
spend our formative years trying to comprehend the confusion
we're forced to ingest.

Therefore we return once more to the question posed at the
beginning of verse one,
Who shapes the flesh, and who shapes the day? To me the
answer is apparent:
I am shaped by the day. Like a computer cursor awaiting the
next response.
Who out there is my antithesis; the programmer that punches in
the question?

Andy 03.09.03

Why Can't You Hear?

Who do you turn to when the walls cave in?
Where do you go when there's nothing left to win?
When the writing on the wall talks only of pain
And you no longer have anything left to give or gain?

Is there no one I can talk to? No one to answer my prayers?
They just look at me and I can't handle their bitter stares.
They think I have all that I could ever hope to achieve
Yet my one greatest wish is denied! The wish to un-conceive!

To the untrained eye there are many people for me to consult
Yet I could not get from them, an untainted, unbiased result.
Too many are too close and all are neck deep in my game
They don't hear, just silence me with their definition of blame

Too many stand and try to teach me just what to do
Yet all their opinions are no good, no single one true!
I sit in the dark and listen with my thoughts in disgrace
To hear them yelling and throwing my troubles in my face!

How much can I take? Why can't you hear?
Why must I sit in silence to hide from my fear?
I have not the strength, nor the ability to fight
And to this day, I still have no idea who is right!

The many faces seem bent on taking me though guilt
The bloody foundations upon which they have built
This little cage where I can be seen, be viewed be reviewed
And they can spit me out all beaten, broken, wasted and chewed!

Andy 14.10.99

Why Did You Go?

Chester, Why did you go?
Fame came so quick, your death so slow
You talked when you sang
We heard but we didn't get it.
Did you try? We cry,
But did we?

Chris, you didn't have to go.
You were there to play to us when we fell
We weren't there when you tried to tell
And so we danced to the tunes
That were your pleas
And we did not hear.

Caroline, I'm sorry
You wanted fame and you earned it
We built you a pyre upon which to sit
They waited until you slipped
Then lit a fire too hot to fight
You tried, they lied, and then... you died.

George, lost and lonely George!
Last Christmas you gave us a song
That carried us through so many years
Families together, giving gifts, giving life.
The media loved to hate and so they pounced
Turned your life into one you could not bear.

Who cares if one more light goes out?
Everything's so heavy, in the end; crawling!
Fell on black days, show me how to live!
No love on this island; Big brother watches
Maybe we're all just praying for time

Freedom; Faith; Can we give it one more try?

I guess in this world of social media and phones, of all you can eat data and playlists no one listens.
How easy is it to ignore the loudest voice
How easy to sift the surface and never see, never hear or never, ever understand.
We hear. We do not listen.

Andy 20.06.20

To anyone looking down the same path. Don't go. There is help, I promise.

Wronged

Why must I work
With hands not my own?
Why must I think
With a mind which is not my own?
Why must I be
That which is not my own?
Too much is not my own!

Is it wrong, I wonder
To act alone, independent
Of outside demands?
Scorned for looking left
When others demand I Turn right.
Faces of anger, turn tear-filled eyes
Away when the independent enters.

The independent!
An unwanted persona
Feared by those it loves.
And it cries for that love.
Yet blind eyes stare back
Unable, unwilling
To accept its own choices.

I cry for you, independent!
I work with hands not my own
I think with a mind, not my own
I am that, which is not my own
I am that independent, so unwanted
By the love it cries in vain for.
The independent, so painfully wronged.

Andy (finished) 17.7.93

About This Author

Andy was born in Clydebank which is located just on the outskirts of Glasgow. Although he has moved around at heart he still identifies himself as a Bankie. He's always had a keen interest in the arts, picking up his first bass guitar at the age of fifteen and then playing in local bands for most of the 1990's. He recorded a series of demos and EPs culminating in a weekly headline slot at The Arena in Glasgow as well as a stint in Nice n Sleazy's.

However, it is his expression through writing which provided the means of escape. His range runs from novels and short stories to the intrinsic and passionate poetry which supported him through many personal tragedies and difficult times. He currently resides in Moodiesburn with his wife and family, which include what he refers to as "the real boss of the house, our ever-loving and ever-demanding Lhassa Apso - Bella".

Other Works By This Author

For The Latest Information On

New Releases

&

Coming Soon

Please Visit

JasamiPublishingLtd.com

Printed in Poland
by Amazon Fulfillment
Poland Sp. z o.o., Wrocław

64945769R00096